Other books by this author:

LAND SPEED RECORD
From 39.24mph to 600+
(with Cyril Posthumus)

THE FASTEST MAN ON EARTH
The inside story of Richard Noble's
Land Speed Record

AUTOMOBILE RECORD
BREAKERS

THE WORLD OF FORMULA 1
(with Alan Henry)

NIGEL MANSELL

THE LAND SPEED RECORD

RACERS APART
Memories of Motorsport Heroes

DAMON HILL
The Legacy of Speed

ECHOES OF IMOLA

FORMULA ONE

DAMON HILL
World Champion

THE SCIENCE OF SPEED
The fascinating high-tech
world of Formula 1

F1.50
A celebration of 50 years of
Formula One Grand Prix Racing

JORDAN

FORMULA 1 RACING TEAM

David Tremayne

DEDICATION
For Rob and Bosco: left behind, but not forgotten.

First published in April 1998

A catalogue record for this book is
available from the British Library

ISBN: 1 85960 417 X

Library of Congress catalog card no. 97-77755

Haynes North America Inc.,
861 Lawrence Drive, Newbury Park,
California 91320, USA.

Published by Haynes Publishing, Sparkford,
Nr Yeovil, Somerset BA22 7JJ, UK.

Tel: 01963 440635 Fax: 01963 440001
Int. tel: +44 1963 440635 Fax +44 1963 440001
E-mail: sales@haynes-manuals.co.uk
Web site: http://www.haynes.com

Designed and typeset by G&M, Raunds, Northamptonshire
Printed and bound in France by Imprimerie Pollina s.a., Lucon, France No. 73336

Contents

Acknowledgements

I enjoyed writing this book very much, because so much of it is about people I like and respect. Of course I'd like to thank Eejay himself, for his friendship, assistance and abuse over the years, even if some sort of blarney damper would have been welcome at times.

I'd like to single out Jordan team race director Trevor Foster and commercial director Ian Phillips, not only for assisting at rudely short notice but for doing so with such candour. And also for being *racers*. The sport needs more of them.

Finally, thanks to Laurence Foster and Mark Skewis, at the time the editors respectively of those essential weekly reads *Autosport* and *Motoring News*, for permission to quote from work I have done for both.

Introduction

When Eddie Jordan took his racing team into Formula 1 for the 1991 season, many paddock cynics sneered and awaited the fall. He was brash, voluble and smart, and had been a whirlwind in the British Formula 3 and European Formula 3000 Championships. On top of that he also had high ambitions – the perfect ingredients to set rivals' nerves on edge.

Some were foolish enough to write

The Jordan team lost no time testing its aggressive and eye-catching new 198, which was in action at Barcelona within days of its launch. (LAT)

him off as something of a wide-boy. But those who had monitored Eddie Jordan Racing's annual development knew that the Irish entrepreneur was going to stick at it, and those who had worked closely with him understood the rare acumen that means the difference between survival and failure.

We have the funds, engine and drivers to give us an edge

In that first season his cars set enviably high standards and were deemed the best-handling in the business, but the effort nearly bankrupted the team. In the second year they were let down by poor engines, yet turned the financial corner. Ever since then, Jordan has made steady progress, each year seeing the cars nibble a little bit closer to the top. In 1997 they could have won their first Grand Prix, with only slightly better fortune.

The 1998 season would be crucial. With excellent funding from Benson & Hedges, powerful engines from Mugen-Honda, a driver line-up of 1996 World Champion Damon Hill alongside the promising Ralf Schumacher, and the team's own maturing confidence, Eddie Jordan and his colleagues firmly believed that they could reach the chequered flag before their rivals on more than one occasion. If so, it would be to generous rejoicing.

Thus it was that when the wraps came off the Jordan 198 Mugen-Honda at London's Albert Hall in mid-January, to the accompaniment of the Cirque du Soleil, Eddie could hardly contain himself.

'I'm not going to get sucked into saying what we can achieve,' he said with a suppressed smile. 'Each year Jordan improves. We are now so close. That's the reason why Damon has come here to join us – to tell us how close. He has this huge wealth of experience that will bring us a new dimension as a team.

'We've done great things in the past on very limited resources. But now we have the funding and the engine package in place, we have a young charger in Ralf, and Damon's experience of winning 21 Grands Prix and the World Championship is of enormous importance to us. It should give us an edge. That's what you are always seeking in F1, and this year I hope that we have truly found it.'

Damon, after a very disappointing 1997 season with Arrows, was also caught up in the pre-season enthusiasm.

'This is an enormously important season for me. The desire is to win. I don't want to make up the numbers. We have to be realistic – challenging for the championship this year will be very difficult But the target is to win a race. I will be very disappointed if we don't achieve that aim.'

Anxious not to express over-optimistic expectations for the year ahead, Eddie Jordan nonetheless left nobody in doubt of his determination to break into the winners' circle in 1998. (Formula 1 Pictures)

When I think of Eddie, it is with a tolerant smile and a headful of vignettes.

There's Eddie Jordan competing in his one and only Formula 2 race at Donington Park back in 1979, two years before our paths first crossed; and doing a respectable job of chasing his mate Stefan Johansson's similar March.

There's the family friendship forged in our years together as team owner and hack in the British F3 Championship – 'expletive editor of an expletive tabloid newspaper!' was how I remember him quaintly describing my profession.

Or the Monday afternoon when he called and I was secretly congratulating myself on getting in the day's first profanities when I realised that instead of laughing down the telephone he was crying. That was when our friend Rob Bowden, Eejay's chief mechanic, had been the innocent victim of tragedy as the Jordan transporter crashed over a cliff on its return from Martin Brundle's successful assault on the F3 race that supported the 1983 Austrian GP. Such moments have a way of tempering relationships.

There's the expression on his face the day in Phoenix in 1991, when we sat together and I congratulated him on officially becoming an F1 team owner and advised him that as of that date our friendship had ceased as he had backed out of a promised deal, and lacked the courage to tell me to my face.

The trouble is, no matter how strong one's resolve, it is impossible to dislike the fellow. Distrust him, yes; dislike him? Not a chance. Eejay is a character, a guy who makes you laugh. One of those people who becomes a part of your life almost without you realising it.

Then there was the time we all had a riotous lunch at Jordan's (no relation) restaurant by Sydney's Darling Harbour, before I sat to watch the wonderful film *The Commitments* sandwiched between Jordan and media colleague Maurice Hamilton, both of whom knew its background city Dublin intimately. Somehow their stereo humour made the film even funnier. I don't doubt that the tinctures we had imbibed over lunch played their part, too. Happy days.

When the Jordan team wins its first Grand Prix there will be a warm feeling, for Eejay and for valued friends within the organisation he has built with such admirable determination and skill. And, assuredly, that day will come and it will be good to let the emotions flow. It is only a matter of time.

David Tremayne
Harrow and Stapleton
February 1998

Chapter 1

Carpets on the Naas Road

Like Frank Williams, the man whose Formula 1 achievements he most aspires to emulate, Edmund Jordan had one massive asset besides total commitment when he took his successful F3000 team into F1: he knew how to do a deal.

Never too proud to ask, cajole or even beg, he would do the most menial tasks if it helped him to achieve his

Jordan the driver. From an early stage Eddie's grasp of sponsorship was already clearly very well developed. (Sutton Motorsport)

As a driver Eejay got as high as Formula 2, racing this March 792 at Donington Park in 1979 before deciding to hang up his helmet. (Sutton Motorsport)

goal. All pride was buried beneath a burning desire to succeed. Over the years, from humble beginnings selling carpets to Saturday and Sunday race-goers on the Naas Road near Dublin, he would parlay his extraordinary innate ability to match supply to demand to build up a team that has become highly respected. But unlike many others who had driven a similar track, he would do so with a mix of blarney, bonhomie, cunning and charisma that leaves those who come in contact with him aware that they have met somebody quite extraordinary.

He remains unusual as a team owner, in so far as he will talk to anyone. Some of his counterparts are far too lofty to spend more than minimal time indulging in everyday pleasantries. Some don't even take the trouble to extend themselves that far. But Jordan is usually around for anyone who wants a business word or just a chat, and will always throw the odd vulgarity in the direction of any passing journalist, driver, team owner or trade representative. He is a true egalitarian. Everyone gets treated the same way, even if it is only to have his integrity, parentage or ability called into the same jocular question. Seven years into his campaign to win a Grand Prix, there are no signs of this endearing (though occasionally wearing) aspect of his larger-than-life personality changing in the slightest.

Like many before him, Eddie Jordan began by driving before settling for the

The 1983 story frequently cast Ayrton Senna as the victor in British F3. Here the Brazilian celebrates another triumph with Martin Brundle (right) and Calvin Fish. By the middle of the season, however, Brundle was a force to be reckoned with in the EJR Ralt. (Formula 1 Pictures)

entrepreneurial side. But if his parents had had their way he might have had to curb his wicked tongue. 'They would have been very happy for me to be a priest,' he confesses. 'And it was a very big thing in my thoughts at one stage. When I was 15 I was sure in my own mind that I had a very serious calling from God to follow that kind of life.'

Jordan was born in Dublin on 30 March 1948, but after leaving Synge Street CB School in 1966 he planned to study dentistry at university. Then he had a calling of a different kind when he opted instead for the world of finance. Some say that there Eejay found his true god, and today, it must be said, it is easier to envisage him

winning his first World Championship than ever it is to picture him as a chaste member of the priesthood.

He worked for the Bank of Ireland in 1967, while simultaneously studying cost and management accountancy at Dublin's College of Commerce. It would all be time very well spent.

The driving started by sheer coincidence. There had been a strike in Dublin in 1970 and he'd gone to work in Jersey that summer for the Jersey Electricity Company. By night he supplemented his income by working in a bar. There he happened on a kart race at Bouley Bay, and later he discovered the little kart track at St Brelades. It wasn't long before he was hooked,

This poignant photo shows Rob Bowden waving the Union flag at Osterreichring as the team celebrates Martin Brundle's GP-support victory. Eddie can just be spotted to the right, while Jim Wright, now with Williams, is the third yellow shirt from the left. A day later, Bowden was killed on the way home. (Formula 1 Pictures)

and much of the money he had earned was immediately reinvested in lapping the circuit. Back in Dublin he bought a 100cc kart, and by 1972 he was national champion. Within two years he'd graduated to Formula Ford 1600 with one of John Crossle's 30F racing cars, and that first season he won several times. By 1975 he had jumped up to Formula 3, but a serious accident with Kenny Gray at Mallory Park in England broke his left leg in several places and brought his racing temporarily to a halt.

Shortly after this Martin Donnelly, the Belfast racer who would play a prominent part in Jordan's subsequent story, recalls the first time he became aware of the man who would so boost his career. 'It was around 1976, before my own racing career began. My father was running a Royale RP26, and after we'd stayed in the Ormond Hotel in Dublin we were driving down this dual carriageway section of the Naas Road, going to Mondello Park. In those days you used to have those Volkswagen pick-ups. You could let the back end down and hold it horizontal with chains, and there was enough room to transport the racing car that way. A lot of teams used them. I remember my father commenting as we drove past this parked pick-up, "that was Eddie Jordan, selling rugs at the side of the road."'

Gary Anderson – Jordan's gentle giant

Gary Anderson's serious motorsport career began at Brabham in 1972, after he'd moved to England from his native Coleraine in Northern Ireland and had a spell as a mechanic with Motor Racing Stables down at Brands Hatch. According to legend he turned up at Brabham looking for Formula 1 work, was in the process of being told there wasn't any, and then impressed everyone with his ability to lift a Cosworth DFV engine single-handed off the back of a delivery truck. He got a job.

By 1974 he had risen to chief mechanic, but design work was beginning to hold his interest and the following year he was helping Gordon Murray with the design of the Alfa Romeo flat-12-powered Brabham BT45. He also gave vent to his aspirations to race by purchasing a second-hand Brabham F3 chassis and running it after penning his own design updates. Dick Parsons raced the car successfully in the British F3 series, for which Anderson designed the original Anson chassis after leaving Brabham in 1977. The company was an amalgamation of his name and that of his wife Jenni's brother, Bob Simpson, with whom he worked. That Anson, and others which would appear in the early 1980s, were elegant and innovative by the standards of F3, but when an Iranian consortium approached asking to buy out the rights to the original car in 1977, they saw the wisdom of accepting.

At the end of that year Anderson joined McLaren, rising quickly to chief mechanic before graduating to second-in-command to chief designer Gordon Coppuck. After further success second time round with Anson – as design/engineering consultant for F1, F3, Super Vee, Group C – he moved to America in 1985 to oversee Rick Galles' Indycar programme, acting as chief engineer and general manager. After a year's sabbatical he was back in the UK by 1987, in charge of the Bromley Motorsport F3000 team. In 1988 he developed and engineered Roberto Moreno's championship-

winning Reynard. A year later Anderson was headhunted by Adrian Reynard as chief designer, responsible for the Bicester constructor's 1990 F3000 challenger. Then he got the F1 call from Jordan.

It was something of a surprise appointment, since Anderson was such a shy character that many people were in ignorance of his true ability. Work began on the design of the 191 in April 1990, and as events would prove, Eddie Jordan had made an inspired choice.

As Jordan's technical director Anderson lives a high-pressure life, but takes his relaxation in a love of narrow boats. It's not just the blessed contrast to the pace of F1 that Anderson finds so appealing. The tranquillity is a valuable prompt for thoughts about the cars he designs. 'You can do a hell of a lot of thinking. I find it very good, because you're away from racing and your mind is so clear.'

'You know, Gary, this is the best F1 car I've ever driven!' Andrea de Cesaris (right) loved the 191, and never tired of telling people. (Formula 1 Pictures)

Jordan never saw himself as above anything that might augment his racing budget or better his standard of living. Donnelly continues: 'He told me himself that he used to sell salmon outside the football ground, or when the big rugby internationals were on. When he got moved on by the coppers, he'd just go to another gate. The old sludger!'

Donnelly, like many who have come within Jordan's orbit, gives as good as he gets when it comes to the banter. But there is underlying affection which robs it of any apparent spite. 'Eddie was always good to me. But my old sponsor, Frank Nolan, a fellow Dubliner and a builder, didn't trust Eejay. Frank died on 13 April 1986, and I honestly believe to this day that if he had lived I would never have had any involvement with Eddie.'

In 1977 Jordan had recovered sufficiently to run rampage in Ireland's Formula Atlantic series with an ex-Alan Jones March, before winning the title a year later in a Chevron B29. He began to consider the British F3 Championship, the country's premier single-seater series, in which there was never any shortage of talent. By 1979 World Champion-to-be Nelson Piquet had only recently graduated to F1, while his sparring partner, Derek Warwick, had moved up to Formula 2, then one step below F1 on the racing ladder. The fresh entries in F3 that season included an ambitious Brummie called Nigel Mansell, who had finally found himself a paid ride in a Unipart March run by Dave Price Racing; an erratic Italian called Andrea de Cesaris, who would later play a key role in Jordan Grand Prix's story; and a

young New Zealand sensation, Mike Thackwell. Not to mention Team Ireland, which was running a pair of Chevron B47s for Eddie Jordan and his friend Stefan Johansson, the Swede.

'Thackwell was the kiddie then,' Jordan laughs now, with the ruefulness of a man who wished he'd signed him to a management deal. 'I thought he was the mega.'

'The mega', 'the crack', 'I own you' (but very definitely not 'I owe you'). These are all expressions – the print-able ones – that typically pepper Eejay's speech. That year he had some reasonable results, but nothing earth-shattering. And he realised he had come to a crossroads:

'I'm not trying to use anything as an excuse for myself. I've been quite lucky in the respect that I wasn't good enough to make it, and my mind told me so at an early enough stage not to be in there hanging on all the time.

'I wanted to stay in the sport, and I felt I could use the experience I'd had as a driver, and the experience I'd had being thrown in the deep end in 1979 to run Derek McMahon Racing in F3, which in itself was difficult.' McMahon was a colourful character whose exploits are said to have included introducing a drunken donkey into a basement disco on one particularly notable Austrian trip, and who ran his own motorsport operations for the likes of Jordan's countrymen Bernard Devaney and Derek Daly.

The financial juggling that Jordan found necessary to keep the thing rolling would ultimately pay dividends when it came to setting up Eddie Jordan Racing in the late 1970s. It operated from a lock-up unit at Silverstone.

Jordan contested F3 from 1981–89, and F3000 from 1985–91.

The F3 operation began with David Sears at the wheel in 1981, and after a front-row start at Thruxton their first race yielded second place. But shortly after that, circumstance put Jordan together with an impoverished but talented Scotsman, David Leslie, whose own programme with a Hope Scott Ralt had finally run out of funds. It was a marriage of convenience for both which Leslie, now a star of the British Touring Car Championship,

As Senna leads into the Thruxton chicane, Brundle gets tough with Davy Jones, fighting to the last breath for the 1983 Marlboro British F3 Championship. The Brazilian took the title, but the season was the making of EJR. (Formula 1 Pictures)

soon rewarded with some good drives and decent results. They didn't have the budget to be championship contenders though, and a damp race at Oulton Park typified their precarious situation. Leslie slithered across the line in fourth place with one of his front tyres flat; this was so old even before the short race that it had literally worn through.

You understood why so many sponsors came under his spell

Jordan gambled again in 1982 when he ran the Englishman James Weaver in a dual campaign in the British series and selected European F3 Championship events. And it paid off (even if jointly they somehow failed to get their entry in on time for the prestigious Monaco F3 support race), because the team gained experience working beyond British club events and of the travel that it entailed.

'I was always keen to broaden my education,' Jordan says. 'If there was an Atlantic race in Hong Kong I would want to be there. Not because I like travelling, because I don't. But I needed to broaden my experience.' Such opportunities all helped to build credibility.

Jordan's best season was 1983, when Martin Brundle staged a fabulous fight with the emergent Ayrton Senna for the British F3 Championship. By refusing to give up, even after losing the first nine races to the brilliant Brazilian, Brundle took the fight to the final round, and won several races along the way. Both he and Eddie Jordan Racing emerged from the season with their credibility high. But it was also the year in which tragedy visited the team. After Brundle had beaten Gerhard Berger in the F3 race that supported the Austrian GP on the very quick Osterreichring circuit, the team's transporter crashed over a cliff on a notoriously tortuous section of nearby road, killing chief mechanic Rob Bowden. Jordan himself was shattered. Friends rallied round, however, urging him not to succumb to the immediate impulse to give it all up. It was an understandable reaction, as any team owner who has plumbed such depths will know, but when he did make the decision to go forward he did it with even greater determination not to squander the investment that Rob had made in helping to shape the team.

In 1990, as he stood on the brink of F1, Jordan still rated one particular race as the team's highest achievement. 'The combined British and European F3 round at Silverstone, the one where Martin and Ayrton opted to run on European rubber, and Allen Berg for the British championship's standard Avon tyres,' he chuckled. 'It was one of our biggest feats, with Martin and Tommy Byrne finishing one-two in the European section and overall, and Allen finishing third over-

Tommy Byrne and his friend Stan Oldacre confer before the start of Silverstone's European F3 Championship round in 1984.
(Formula 1 Pictures)

After winning his first F3000 race for EJR in Spain earlier in the season, Herbert staged a scintillating drive from last to third place at Monza. (Sutton Motorsport)

all and first in the British section. We finished first and second and first in the same race with three cars, and Martin beat Ayrton fair and square that day . . .'

Jordan's dream to graduate to F3000, which had replaced F2 as the final rung before F1, was born from this F3 springboard. But initially it would bring Eddie Jordan Racing down to earth with a damaging bump. By his own admission, 1985 would be his most cathartic season to date.

'We went backwards for the first time, and it stopped me,' he confesses. 'It was a bad year, a very bad year. It almost brought us to our knees. There were still the big names in F3 – Dick Bennetts and West Surrey Racing, Dave Price – it was very, very difficult for us to attract the right sort of

people.' In conversations such as this Jordan's voice drops a couple of octaves, the way it does when he really wants to make a point. As if he has suddenly adopted you as his confessor. You feel privy to something very secret. 'We were struggling,' he imparts, as though this had not been all too obvious from watching the action out on the track. You could feel your heart warming to his problems, and begin to understand why so many unsuspecting sponsors have succumbed to his blandishments over the years.

'We did F3000 on nothing close to the right money. We put on a reasonable show for Thierry Tassin, a good show, and he did a lot of work. At the end of the year we finished third with Claudio Langes in Curacao and we had an outside chance to win it. But to

22

finish in the top three of the last race of the F3000 Championship that year – that brought us the credibility.

'F3000 was a steep learning curve, though I wasn't sure at the time that it wasn't as steep as we were estimating the curve would be, learning in F1.' F1 would be more difficult he later conceded, then couldn't help adding, 'but then again, sometimes I think that maybe it won't be.' It was a typically enthusiastic comment from a man who

The severity of the accident that befell Johnny at Brands Hatch in 1988 is evident here, moments after his second impact. (Sutton Motorsport)

Jean Alesi: From animal changes to F3000 title

Jean Alesi went to Jordan at the end of 1988 in a parlous state after a frustrating year with the French Oreca team. He had effectively been dropped from Marlboro's sponsorship umbrella and was facing an inglorious end to a once promising career. Everyone bar Eddie Jordan seemed to have written him off.

'For me it was a very tough time,' Jean recalls. 'This is a game where you don't get too many chances, and of course I was scared that mine had all gone. I knew what I could do, and I was just desperate for the chance to prove it. Eddie gave me that, and I shall always be grateful.'

The team's first test at Vallelunga went a long way towards calming Alesi's fears. In the 1988 EJR Reynard he was faster than Pacific Racing's 1989 cars, and faster than Donnelly. 'I knew how much that test mattered to me, and I just drove that car as fast as I possibly could. That did a lot for my confidence.'

Legend has it that Alesi lived as family with Eddie Jordan, but in fact he stayed for a week or so initially while Eddie found him a room to let with a couple in Oxford. 'He lived there for a couple of months,' Trevor Foster says. 'In the early days his English was poor and his brother Jose used almost to interpret for him, but gradually it improved. At that stage he was also very tense, and he was obsessed with beating Eric Bernard, with whom he had fought all

through the junior formulae. They were both vying for the accolade of best upcoming Frenchman, but we told him he had 26 drivers to beat, not one. We did everything we could as a team to break the taboo that existed in France, that it was dangerous for a Frenchman to race with an English team, especially with an English team-mate.

'Jean remained tense until he won at Pau. After that he calmed down visibly. He went back to live in France then, and commuted to races. You could tell how relaxed he had become because he just used to tell us he was happy if Martin did all the testing. He'd just tune his car when he got to the races.

'His worst trait was clutchless gearchanges in qualifying. We had to put new gears and dog-rings in the gearbox every time. I said to him once, "Jean, can't you get them to last better than that? Can't you use the clutch?" He replied, "But it's worth two tenths of a second if I don't use it!" So he just did animal changes. We needed new gears and rings for the races too, but in those he would use the clutch, and everything was okay.'

Alesi remembers his time with Jordan fondly. 'It was a happy team, and they played very fair with me. I had equal equipment to Martin, and that is all a driver has any right to ask. Winning the 1989 Formula 3000 Championship with Eddie was one of my best achievements. I learned a lot.'

Having been rescued by Eddie Jordan for 1989, Jean Alesi had much to celebrate en route to winning EJR the F3000 crown. (Sutton Motorsport)

can only ever think positively. But Eddie Jordan would discover that the learning curve in F1 would indeed be far steeper than anything he had ever encountered in F3 or F3000.

'It all made me ask myself some very, very serious questions,' he admits of that poor 1985 season. 'Almost the same sort I'd asked myself in 1980. Was I good enough to continue? And it was a fairly close-run thing. This time I came out and said, yes, I have the ability, and I need to give it another show. But I've got to get off my arse and push myself harder because we're not performing.'

You learn a lot about people when they are in adversity. Once again Jordan rallied his F3 troops around the speedy and extremely polished little Brazilian, Maurizio Sandro Sala, to try to undo the harmful and expensive season of accidents and disappointments he had suffered with the Norwegian Harald Huysman and Australian rookie Steve Harrington in 1985. Part of the problem had been the arrival of Adrian Reynard's innovative carbon-fibre Reynard chassis. In a formula in which psychology is vitally important, the Reynard had initially wiped the floor with the trusty Ralts that had been the category's mainstay, and to which Jordan had remained faithful and would continue to be faithful for the 1986 season. Working with engineers Dave Benbow and Paul Heath, Sala challenged Andy Wallace and Madgwick Motorsport for the title, and though EJR ultimately was beaten,

it brought the team back its self-respect. Motivation was high again.

A year later Thomas Danielsson turned down the number one seat in an F3 EJR Reynard-Spiess, and Johnny Herbert, who was initially to have been the Swede's number two, stepped into the breach and won the championship. EJR was back on the right track.

In April 1988 Herbert won his, the team's and Reynard's maiden F3000 race in Jerez, Spain. In August he was challenging for the championship when his career was threatened following a horrendous accident with Gregor Foitek and Olivier Grouillard at Brands Hatch. Herbert's feet were so badly smashed that the doctors considered amputation – certainly everyone

believed his driving (and perhaps even walking) days were over. It was a devastating blow for all concerned. But a sign of Eddie Jordan Racing's growing strength was that Herbert's team-mate, Martin Donnelly, was able to win the re-started race, win again at Dijon before the season ended, and finish third in the championship. The team was reaching professional maturity.

Donnelly was another beneficiary of Eddie Jordan Management, the business Jordan set-up with his friend and legal adviser, Fred Rodgers. The Ulsterman had signed a six-year contract at one stage: 'It was when I was up against the wall and my career was dying on its feet. Thomas Danielsson lost his licence for a while because of an eye problem, and I signed a management contract with EJM to partner Johnny. My attitude then was that to give 15 per cent of nothing – because I was going nowhere – was a good deal and I'd be willing to give up the money for it. Fifteen per cent wasn't a bad deal. In F3000 I did those five races at the end of 1988; I won that race in which Johnny was hurt, had another win, two seconds and retired while leading the other one. At the end of 1988 Lotus was on about signing me as its second driver in F1 . . .'

In 1986 Donnelly had established himself as a strong contender in F3, winning four races and finishing third overall in the rankings. The following year, after a difficult start, he won the

Jordan's ambience helped turn Eddie Irvine into an F3000 winner under the Camel banner in 1990. (Formula 1 Pictures)

prestigious Macau Grand Prix despite near-typhoon conditions. But his progress had then stalled at the beginning of 1988 when he was obliged to stay in F3 for a third year. By midseason, feeling thoroughly jaded, he jumped ship, joining Jordan's Q8 F3000 team. This was a lifeline that set in train one of those remarkable turnarounds that drivers dream of. It put Donnelly's career right back on track.

If Eddie could pull strokes, however, so could Donnelly. 'By the end of 1988 Eddie had realised he wasn't getting a string of money coming in, because I'd told him that Rio Nolan, Frank's widow, was going to be paying when I knew she wasn't. Eddie thought she would be paying £30,000 because I'd sold him on believing it. So he sold me off to Vern Schuppan to drive his Porsche 962 sportscar at Spa and then in Japan, and in 1989 Eddie was my pimp.'

He was a damn good one. He got Donnelly a drive with Tokyo R&D in Japan, a test contract with Lotus, and a deal to do the Daytona 24 Hour endurance race for TWR and the Le Mans classic for Nissan. It was all excellent experience for a hungry driver, but by far the most important step was when Jordan got him into the Arrows F1 team for the French GP after regular driver Derek Warwick had hurt himself in a kart race in Jersey. (Eddie had also got Jean Alesi, now a member of his F3000 squad, into a Tyrrell for the 1989 French GP

Heinz-Harald Frentzen, however, was inconsistent though fast in the team's third Reynard 90D. (Formula 1 Pictures)

and the rest of that season.)

'So I made my F1 debut, and there wasn't a free weekend,' Donnelly smiles. 'And then I did Macau again at the end of that year.' This all led on directly to the drive alongside Warwick at Team Lotus for 1990. 'Obviously my exceptional talent got me in there,' he chuckles. 'But I think it was because I had done enough in 1989 to show them that I was worthy of the seat, and Fred Rodgers helped me to negotiate it.'

If Eejay did a deal for you he'd always make money on it too

It wasn't all plain sailing, however, as Donnelly recalls: 'In 1990 Eddie gave me a contract which was all very much me, me, me, me, me. All on his side. I said, "Eejay, it's got to be worth my while to take me away from a second year at Lotus. You've got to match somewhere near the financial contents of that, and I'd like good testing and all the rest of it."

'Then he produced a second contract, which was a little bit more acceptable, and then he came up with another one which we were able to agree terms on. So he was still my manager then. Of course, he wanted to take his commission off the money he was paying me! I said, "Eejay, catch yourself on. You're paying me money with one hand, and on the other hand you're taking it back again!" But it was

good. I enjoyed the wheeling and dealing with him.'

Donnelly was one of the few people known to have got the better of a deal with Jordan, back in late 1988. 'It went from me having to pay Eddie that £30,000, which obviously I hadn't got. I hadn't got two pence! And ended with him paying me fifty grand to drive for him the following year. Plus, plus, plus! That was a bloody good deal! I did all the negotiation. There was Trevor Foster saying to Eddie to do it and they were at it all day long. Then Eddie came out and said, "That's it, Fred! I'm pissed off. He's just having a laugh! Get somebody else up here!" And there were Trevor and Fred saying, "Oh God, Martin, you're upsetting him!" And this went on all day. They called it the winter of discontent.

'You had to accept in life that if a deal was being done on your behalf by Eejay, then he would make money on it. You had to accept that. You'd also make money for yourself, but Eejay would always make money out of it. And if you couldn't accept that, he'd mess up your head. He always was a wheeler-dealer. A very good and very shrewd wheeler-dealer. And Eejay today is successful in life because he's a very good talker, he's a very good politician and he gets good people around him. I consider him a good friend.'

In 1989 Alesi won the European F3000 Championship for Eddie Jordan Racing, with Donnelly in eighth position. The time for the big move to F1 was fast approaching.

With Eddie Jordan you know that whatever time you schedule for an interview is only an estimate. A basis for negotiation. Just as you also know that you might talk for 10 minutes, 15 if you're really lucky, before he takes the inevitable telephone call. The interruption then initiates a comical scenario, where Jordan alternately wheedles and cajoles, then demands and bullies, as the conversation ebbs and flows with frequent abusive joshing. At times he can be harder to pin down than a dollar bill in a hurricane, though that is a trick many believe he alone could perfect.

Jordan's background knowledge of his sport is lamentable. He may know everyone who has ever moved within it since his own interest was fired, but history eludes him. How else to explain that he once thought the great 1930s ace Bernd Rosemeyer was a tennis player?

To everyone he is Eddie or, more frequently, Eejay. But he is never Mr Jordan. Formality is anathema to the man who, lunching at Sydney's Darling Harbour, offended sponsors' wives by continually pointing his famous wagging finger down the table at Jean Alesi and observing at high volume: 'I expletive own you, you expletive lowlife Formula 3000 deadbeat. I made you and I took you in 1989 when nobody else wanted you, and don't you ever forget it! You're mine!'

This was of course all said with a big smile and, as with most of his comments, intended as a wind-up. Vulgar indeed it was, but it says much for his character that by the end of lunch even the wives were laughing (or at least smiling) with him. He may not be everybody's cup of tea, and for sure he is no shrinking violet, nor the sort of boy many girls might have dared take home to meet Mum and Dad. His wife Marie, a tower of strength in the background, was braver than most as befits one who could swim and play netball to Olympic standards. Theirs is a very close relationship, and they have four children, Zoe, Miki, Zak and Kyle.

When a sponsor presentation or media launch calls for it, Jordan can lay on the hype as effusively as the next man, and for many years it was a standing joke that his pre-season launch speech would always include the promise of the team's first victory. But in private he has been shrewdly candid in assessing matters. As he stood on the brink of F1 back in 1990, he again took stock of the situation. 'As a team we have planned over the period of almost a generation, 10 years. We started off well in 1980 but then 1985 was the dip. That was when it was either going to stop, or else pull itself back up the graph. And Sala helped it to do just that, he helped drag it back up. And once the pendulum was swinging in our favour again, Johnny was able to take it on from there.'

And so Eddie Jordan steered his little team towards F1, upsetting people with their own vested interests along the way but looking only to the front like the speedboat pilot on the Thames who doesn't give another thought to the dirty wake he is creating which upsets others punting along the river.

In the years to come the faster he went, the rougher that wake would be for those left behind to ride it.

Chapter 2

'Welcome to the Piranha Club'

'How can you say when it began, because the dream was there all the time,' Eddie Jordan says when you ask him when his aspiration to go F1 was really born. 'It may have been dormant because it wasn't relevant, but it was always there.

'I thought I could get there once as a driver. In the earlier stages when I was a champion in karting in Ireland, and then quick in Formula Ford, won a number of races, then won a championship in Atlantic, you have this dream. You feel, "Hey, given a chance I might even do it." But a hard season on not a brilliant budget in F3 in Britain and Europe is a great leveller. It opens your eyes wide. You don't know the circuits, the team, and you're up against the top guys.' The 1979 season, when he ran in the British F3 Championship, proved his own turning point, his personal moment of truth that led him instead to team management.

'When I started my first day in F3000, just as in F3 or Formula Ford, F1 was at the back of my mind,' he admits. 'At that stage I was preparing myself, because the reason we made ourselves strong is that we broadened our horizons at an early stage.' Sound advice for those with similar aspirations to progress through the racing ranks.

An inveterate gambler, Jordan had nonetheless studied the odds very, very carefully. 'On pure business,' he said back in 1990, as his friend and former F1 star John Watson tested the first Jordan F1 car at a damp Silverstone, 'I believe I am as good as anyone in F1, with the possible exception of Bernie Ecclestone, because Bernie is a classic. But I think my mind works in a similar way. I started with nothing, so to wind up with nothing is not a big deal. I'm

It's almost certainly not a cheque that Eejay is signing, but the phone is real enough in this 1990 shot taken at EJR's old Silverstone base. (Formula 1 Pictures)

not motivated by money, I'm motivated by success.'

But by the end of his first year in F1, he had not just come very close to ending up with nothing. He faced debts of £4.5 million.

Behind the new enterprise lay a potentially catastrophic reversal of fortune that might well have jeopardised the entire project. It would certainly have deflected anyone less determined. Jordan believed he had been promised serious funding from a major sponsor, but the sponsor ultimately disagreed.

When Johnny Herbert had won the opening round of the European F3000 Championship at Jerez early in 1988, Jordan had already taken typically opportunistic advantage of the young British driver's pole position to do a quick deal to slap Camel stickers on the car. And the victory gave him the ammunition to persuade the R.J. Reynolds tobacco company to stump up title sponsorship on the Herbert car for the remainder of the season. It was EJ enterprise at its zenith, not to mention sheer commonsense. In motor racing you strike while the iron is hot. Or if you are really smart, you strike even while it's warming up.

The following season, with Jean Alesi, Camel-EJR won the European F3000 Championship. It was the team's biggest success, and Camel's first big news since it had come into motorsport.

There had been doubts that Jordan had secured his Ford HB customer engine deal, but it was there for all to see when the new car was first unveiled. (Formula 1 Pictures)

The driver academy

Eddie Jordan Racing, Eddie Jordan Management and Jordan Grand Prix have all acted over the years as one glorified driver academy, nurturing fresh talent and giving it the chance to flourish. Jordan's books over the years read like a motor racing Who's Who. No fewer than eight of the 1998 F1 drivers have driven for him.

In the F3 and F3000 years there were stars such as James Weaver, future F1 star Martin Brundle, Allen Berg, Tommy Byrne, Davy Jones, David Hunt, Harald Huysman, Maurizio Sandro Sala, future F3000 and F1 winner Johnny Herbert, Paul Warwick; in F3000 Thierry Tassin, Russell Spence (one of the great lost talents), Thomas Danielsson, future F1 racer Martin Donnelly, future F1 winner Jean Alesi, future F1 World Champion Damon Hill, future F1 winner Heinz-Harald Frentzen, and Emanuele Naspetti; and in F1 Marco Apicella, future Indycar champion Alex Zanardi, Mauricio Gugelmin, Stefano Modena, Rubens Barrichello, Kelvin Burt (whose so-called test contract wasted his latent talent), future Ferrari racer Eddie Irvine, Giancarlo Fisichella, Ralf Schumacher and Pedro de la Rosa.

Michael Schumacher was the greatest of all of these racers, but he wasn't the only star to elude Jordan. Another was Ayrton Senna, whose first test in an F3 car came courtesy of EJR in 1982. And then in the winter of 1996 Nigel Mansell hauled himself from retirement to test a 196 at Barcelona, fuelling media speculation of a possible return. Though this was always denied, it was clear the former World Champion wasn't doing it purely as a health kick. 'Nigel would have loved to drive, consequent to him feeling within himself that he was committed and determined to do it,' Eddie insists.

'He had retired, there was a gap, and we tested because he asked to have a test. It was a super thing from a commer-

cial and promotional aspect for the team. My impression at the time was that there was a small element of a request to start racing again, but we never ever talked terms or financial things.'

If a driver of Mansell's speed and experience had raced the competitive 197, who knows what might have happened?

Always quick and several times a winner, James Weaver did much to establish the credibility of Eddie Jordan Racing with his performances in the British and European F3 Championships in 1982. (Formula 1 Pictures)

But when R.J. Reynolds announced at the Hungarian GP in August 1990 that it would be switching its sponsoring allegiance from Team Lotus to Benetton's Grand Prix efforts for 1991, Jordan had already heard alarm bells. Worse still, there would also be a measure of support for Williams too. Jordan knew that wasn't going to leave anything in the kitty for his own outfit. He wasn't around F1 paddocks at the time, and asked a journalist to put the hard question to W. Duncan Lee, the company's director of sponsorships and special events: hadn't support been pledged to Jordan?

In his public announcement Lee began by outlining the commitment to Benetton as the sponsorship passed from Lotus, then the support that Williams could expect. But when asked whether he could expand on where Jordan fitted into the plan, and whether it was true that support had been promised, the smoothness of Lee's oratory dried up. 'Not at this time,' was his only comment. Later, in private, he denied that any such agreement with Jordan had ever existed. Jordan took a different view.

'We were guaranteed money with an

'Why didn't you sign me to drive, Eddie?' Jean Alesi and Jordan indulge in a little horseplay early in 1991. Since their success in 1989 they had remained close, though Alesi has never since driven for the team. (Formula 1 Pictures)

existing sponsor, and that's what made it easier to press the button to green, to move from a paper car to a real car.'

Perhaps he had read too much into the situation; perhaps he had been let down. It's always difficult to ascertain such truths in F1 unless you are privy to the inside information at first hand. But certainly Jordan had been pressing Lee very hard all through the 1989 season, when he had serious aspirations to take over the ailing Lotus team.

Back in 1980 a marriage of necessity had been brokered, by John Hogan of sponsor Marlboro, between the struggling McLaren team and Ron Dennis's

emergent Project Four venture. Project Four had just won the British F3 Championship and was building John Barnard's innovative carbon-fibre F1 car as a prelude to its own graduation, whereas McLaren had been running out of steam since James Hunt's last-ditch victory in the 1976 World Championship. McLaren International was thus formed, and it was a long time before anyone looked back.

Eddie Jordan, meanwhile, was very much looking forward. He commissioned a series of reports on the history and state of Lotus as he sought to persuade Lee to act as marriage broker

A family man at heart

For all that he behaves like a human whirlwind, Eddie Jordan remains at heart a family man, and his wife and children have always been an anchor. Marie travels regularly to the races, never intruding but always radiating her own unmistakable presence and adding a quiet air of credibility and dignity. She is as much a part of motorhome life as her husband.

Eddie loves golf, and plays as much as he can out on Sotogrande, but not, apparently, too often with Marie who is an extremely competent player. Equally he adores music. Jordan parties have long been legendary for the quality of their music and their decibels, and more often than not the boss dons a headband and grabs for the drumsticks. He's good too, and always an intrinsic part of the post-British GP rock bash which he organises every year.

The person Eejay most likes talking to is his wife, Marie, who has been a quiet tower of strength and common sense every step of the way. (Darren Heath/LAT)

in a similar deal. This had a lot to recommend it, but for a variety of reasons never happened. He would have to wait a while longer for his chance of greatness.

Already, he was finding F1 a different world. As he struggled to discover a route to the sport's upper echelon, Jordan was like a spirited fish writhing on a hook, twisting and turning any which way as he sought an advantage. But his persistence and refusal to be cowed eventually won through. The new Jordan 191 was unveiled late in 1990.

'Politically, F1 is so different,' he observed. 'So many people can be nice to your face and then slag you off. I don't mean that nastily; some people have been very helpful and kind. I'm trying to do this without causing problems to myself or anyone else. There was no back-stabbing to get the engines, for example.' But there was plenty of speculation that the deal to use Ford's customer HB engine might not go ahead, or might head elsewhere.

When he had some time earlier been in a position to show the monocoque chassis of the sleek new 191, Jordan had been in his usual irrepressible form. 'I've taken a lot of flak recently, with speculation that the Larrousse team is going to take over the Ford engine deal and things like that,' he beamed. 'Well, here's the car, and it says we are going ahead with our F1 project and that we will have the Ford

Jordan's first World Championship points came with de Cesaris' fourth place in Canada, in June 1991. (Formula 1 Pictures)

HB V8. What more can I say?'

It had been a massive struggle just to get the car built, but there it was in the fibre and the metal. But 911, or 191? Thereby hung another tale. Originally the type number was intended to refer to 91, the year, and 1, the category. But Porsche was unhappy, since it had registered 911 for its famous production sportscar models. It is said that an accommodation was reached whereby Eejay changed the design numbering system to 191; and for some 12 months thereafter he was seen driving round in a nice black Porsche. A 911, of course.

That first season saw Gary Anderson's beautiful car win praise and design awards, and Alain Prost expressed the opinion that it was the best-handling car. Team Seven Up Jordan sailed through the mandatory prequalifying for the rabbit teams, held at the crack of dawn on Friday mornings, and by the fifth race, the Canadian GP in Montreal, drivers Andrea de Cesaris and Bertrand Gachot had scored points for fourth and fifth places respectively. It was a highly impressive start.

At 32, de Cesaris was a man of fearsome reputation, and at the time boasted 33 accidents from 150 races. Many of them had come in the Italian's first season with McLaren 10 years before Eejay is thought to have taken advantage of the Marlboro funding that kept his career alive. But Andrea

The writing on the road in Belgium presaged the beginning of a troubled period, after Gachot had been jailed in England for attacking a London cabbie. (Formula 1 Pictures)

had also finished second in Germany and South Africa in 1983 for Alfa Romeo, for whom he had led at Long Beach the previous year, and then come within a few litres of victory at Monaco before running short of fuel. Rumours said he had been allowed up to three Jordan tubs before he would be shown the door. 'Those stories are bullshit!' he laughed.

F1 had a new star, and he was driving a Seven Up Jordan!

For all this background, de Cesaris knew F1 cars. 'I think this is the best car I ever had,' he said of the 191. 'The way I see the car is built, the way I see the effort everyone has put in, shows me signs. Maybe it is not a winning car at the moment, because McLaren and Ferrari and Williams and Benetton are so strong, and for sure I don't think Eddie is expecting to win straight away, but I think we have all the things at the maximum. This for sure is the best racing car I have ever driven. And it is good to be driving for a British team because here, unlike Italy, there is no shortage of experienced people on the engineering side.'

Later that year Andrea ran as high as second in the Belgian GP at Spa. This was a difficult but momentous race for the team. There was the backlash of Belgian anger after Gachot had been imprisoned in Britain, days after setting fastest lap in the Hungarian GP,

for squirting mace in the eyes of a London taxi driver following a traffic altercation. Then another Belgian, Philippe Adams, brought an injunction against the team on the Friday, following a previous disagreement with Eddie Jordan Racing in F3000. Bernie Ecclestone intervened to smooth things over. Behind the scenes there were the growing rumours of the Yamaha deal for 1992.

By half distance de Cesaris was fighting for second with Nelson Piquet's Benetton and Riccardo Patrese's Williams, in Senna's wake. By lap 33 the flying Italian was only 3.3 seconds behind the Brazilian, and charging. But Andrea knew his water temperature was climbing. 'He called in on the radio to tell us,' Anderson said. 'I told him I didn't want to hear about it, and to keep going until the thing broke!' Sadly, that's just what it did, with three laps to go.

That race was memorable for another reason – the arrival of Michael Schumacher in F1. In a Jordan. There was something poignant about the fact that Germany's great new hope should burst forth at Spa, the circuit that took the life of his countryman Stefan Bellof

In the build-up to the Belgian GP Jordan had already been in deep conversation with Jochen Neerpasch, one of Michael Schumacher's many advisers. (LAT)

The upshot was the arrival of F1's latest superstar, as the young German stood in for the incarcerated Gachot. (LAT)

Schumacher quickly demonstrated not just his innate balance in the paddock, but his speed on the track as he qualified seventh. (LAT)

six years earlier in the 1000km sportscar race. And laughable, in hindsight, that Eddie at one stage favoured the idea of letting Stefan Johansson stand in for Gachot, rather than an untried rookie such as Schumacher.

The previous week, in his first F1 drive, testing on the South Circuit at Silverstone, Schumacher had been instantly and devastatingly fast, so much so that Foster and Anderson had tried to slow him down until they saw just how at ease he was. 'We had to tell him to calm down after four laps but by the fifth he beat Stefano Modena's time in the Tyrrell,' Trevor recalls. 'It was as if he had been in the car all season.'

The German had only ever lapped Spa once before free practice began, and that was on his pushbike, but after showing great speed throughout practice he qualified a sensational seventh. From scepticism, Eddie Jordan could now barely believe his good fortune. F1 had a new star in its midst, and he was driving one of the emerald green Seven Up Jordans.

'I'm very happy to have qualified so high, but a lot of it was due to the efforts of the team,' Schumacher beamed. He was young, only 22, and while he was relaxed he also seemed rather cowed by the sheer level of attention his brilliant performance had attracted. Gratefully he accepted an

In the car Schumacher stunned the Jordan engineers with the clarity of his feedback and the calmness of his approach. (LAT)

offer that a planned interview be postponed until the following morning; it never did take place because he didn't turn up. Eddie Jordan, hugging himself, looked like a cat who had discovered a cream factory, but soon he would find that Michael Schumacher was not always where you expected him to be.

The race began as an anti-climax for Jordan. Schumacher did a drag race start to go from seventh to fourth before the clutch succumbed. 'He gave it megadeath,' Eejay said. 'He wasn't fazed by the company up there. What a start!' It was, ironically, the only one Michael Schumacher would make in a Jordan.

After de Cesaris' subsequent retirement the Schumacher phenomenon became a comforter, albeit only temporarily. 'He has a very strong future,' grinned Foster. 'I think so far he has been exceptional. He's very natural, gives good feedback and isn't too technical. He just says do this, do that, and then goes out and is quick again.'

Somebody else was impressed. In the post-qualifying conference Senna was asked for an opinion of the young German's performance. 'He obviously did a very good job, and his place is something special,' he said. And then, indicating that he had already taken

This is Michael Schumacher's first ever GP start, at Spa Francorchamps in 1991. Sadly it lasted little more than a mile as he burned out the clutch in the sprint to the La Source hairpin. (Formula 1 Pictures)

on board another factor in his never-ceasing search for dominance, he added: 'I don't know much about his background . . . yet.'

But he would. They all would. And very soon.

After Spa the F1 world looked forward to seeing the new star out again for Jordan at Monza, but by the time everyone got there all hell was breaking loose. He'd gone to Benetton!

'After Spa we were unbelievably excited,' Jordan said, and Schumacher had done another 300km in the car at Silverstone. But then came the stunning news that his managers Willi Weber and Jochen Neerpasch had done a deal with Flavio Briatore and Tom Walkinshaw at Benetton, after the eagle-eyed Walkinshaw had seen

the chance to grab what was clearly the hottest driver to hit F1 since Senna. It was internecine F1 warfare at its zenith, with Jordan and Fred Rodgers convinced they had their man tied up, and Briatore and Walkinshaw equally sure that they had him. Meanwhile, deposed Benetton driver Roberto Moreno was looking for an injunction against the team dropping him.

The whole situation was very sordid, but eventually Ecclestone intervened again, and by the time free practice began on Friday at Monza, Michael Schumacher was a Benetton driver and Jordan was left to rue what might have been. The German would continue on an ever-ascending curve – but just consider what might have happened had he been forced to drive a Jordan-Yamaha in 1992. Oh how the course of history might have been changed!

The capture at such an early stage of a talent as prodigious as Schumacher's was something that every team owner dreams of, for he single-handedly could have helped to garner the sort of results that attract sponsors. As a small team Jordan could never have afforded to employ a recognised star of similar talent, but to have nurtured your own, almost by mistake . . .

Having to come to terms with the fact that he had got away, that he had not been as tightly tied to the team as Jordan and Rodgers so firmly believed, was therefore incredibly difficult. Ron Dennis summed it all up very succinctly when he said to Eddie: 'Welcome to the Piranha Club.'

Not long after this blow the new Jordan factory was ready for inhabitation towards the end of 1991. Then a greater tragedy struck. Bosco Quinn was a slim, bearded Irishman who had been with Eddie for some years, work-

With Schumacher gone, de Cesaris came through to boost Jordan's morale with a storming drive which took him as high as second place behind Senna, before a fractured water pipe overheated his Ford HB engine. (Formula 1 Pictures)

ing first on the racing side and, latterly, overseeing the factory project. One night just before Christmas he bade goodbye after another long day and headed home. He never made it. His car was struck by another and he was killed outright, at the peak of his achievement within the team.

However bad the cash crisis, he always paid the staff properly

'It was 19 December,' Foster recalls with sadness. 'Down the road here, in Blisworth. I was one of the last people to see him and had spoken to him half an hour before he left. He was just going to check up and look round, and was killed on the way home. Bosco was team manager of the F3 team in 1987 to 1989, and in that role he was sort of factory manager. On an administration basis he was Eddie's right-hand man. There were the three of us, and that's how Eejay got it going. Part of Bosco's project in 1991, when we stopped doing F3 and F3000, was to oversee construction of the factory.

'Funnily enough, he'd bought himself a genuine gypsy caravan at the beginning of 1991, and he wanted to stop with us because he felt it wasn't really what he wanted to do, although he felt that he'd been aiming for it like Eddie had for all those years. He wanted to go and trek off round Europe. We had persuaded him to stay on for one more year and see how it went. I had several conversations with him at the end of 1991, when he said there were things he'd done that he'd wanted to do, and that now he wanted to take time out and travel. And then tragically he was killed. He was a great loss.'

In that first season the make-up of the team was already beginning to change, with the metamorphosis of Eddie Jordan Racing into Jordan Grand Prix. 'We managed to put together a good group of people, and literally in many ways it was against the odds,' Foster says. 'What I liked most of all, which I still miss now, is that the team could go out to dinner. Nowadays, if you want to go out to dinner at a race with the team, it's a major event. You've almost got to take over the restaurant. In those days you could eat most evenings together and there were eight or nine people. And it was good, because most people wanted to eat together. So I miss that.

'There's one thing I will always say for Eddie. There was one time, in the early days of 1991, when things were amazingly difficult. And again in the winter of 1991–92 it was also very bleak for us after we'd struggled to make it through the year. But the first thing Eddie always said to the accountant was, "Right, take the wages out of the bank account first. What've we got left? We'll pay the suppliers and then go and do whatever we have to do."

'And that was his first priority, to be

One race later, Schumacher had jumped ship to Benetton, leaving former Benetton driver Roberto Moreno to ponder the vagaries of F1 fate. (Formula 1 Pictures)

honest, pay the staff. Unlike all the companies who have always done the opposite and gone testing or done this and then done that, and then turned to the staff and said, "Sorry, we can't pay you this month." Eddie always made sure, and to this day I don't think there is any member of staff who can honestly say that they've missed a pay day. I think that's quite an achievement that you can never ever take away from him.

We want to add handsomely to the F1 show in general

'I mean, in that winter of '91 things were so difficult that we were having to ring the bank up and say, "We're putting this cheque through." And the guy was saying, "Okay, I'll honour it." And the understanding with the bank was that if we didn't ring through to say we were writing a cheque, they wouldn't have honoured it. They all had to have a previous phone call, that was the agreement through that winter.'

This was the stickiest time of all for Jordan, when it came closest to going under and joining all the other wrecks that litter the floor of the F1 ocean. But help was also at hand from another source, one with an interest in seeing such professionally run teams surviving: Bernie Ecclestone, the ultimate powerbroker of F1.

'I do believe that Eddie got an advance on certain fees that were due to us in 1992,' Foster admits cautiously. 'It wasn't anything other than that. I don't know the full details, but I believe Bernie advanced the money as a loan to help keep us going, though it had to be paid back, of course.'

Jordan at least knew that he wasn't the only one swimming against the tide. Although that made it tough this also meant that there could be others who ended up weaker. Others who might go to the wall before he did.

'I think it's very difficult for many teams, economically and socially,' he said at the time. 'But where I think we will survive is that we are small, we are used to working within small budgets in F3 and F3000, so the big "spend at all costs" usual F1 type of thing won't apply. We can get through and survive, I think, without that problem. There is no fat, just a lot of hard work, but we've been through all that before here.

'We never expected F1 to be too easy, but what we want to be and what we will be is competitive. We want to look very professional in terms of appearance, presentation and service, and to be a welcome member within the F1 ranks in terms of all the points I've made. We want to add handsomely to the show in general.'

By that yardstick, although as this book went to press the maiden F1 victory had yet to be bagged, Jordan Grand Prix has been a winner all the way. Even in the worst moments of financial crisis it has always main-

Motor racing is a team game, as the sea of green on the pit wall testifies. (Formula 1 Pictures)

Another star that Jordan nurtured, only to discard, was Alessandro Zanardi, seen here at the Japanese GP in 1991. The Italian would go on to dominate IndyCar Racing in 1996 and '97. (Formula 1 Pictures)

tained the highest professional standards and appearance. That in itself says much, not just for Eddie Jordan, but for the spirit he has imbued in his staff.

Back in those early days he had outlined the seriousness of his aspirations. 'Nothing is going to stop us going to F1. I made a commitment based on previous agreements which haven't been honoured. That has hurt us, and we have lost other sponsors because of the identity of the original sponsor. It was a good commitment, and they have told me recently that I should stop, but that would only suit their needs. They fail to understand mine.'

But gradually they all would. He would make them understand.

Chapter

Riding the merry-go-round

In many senses today's F1 team is only as strong as its engine package, most other things being equal. And a supply deal with a manufacturer is an essential part of the delicate winning equation over the long-term. Williams proved this conclusively as far back as 1988, when its supply of Honda engines had dried up and it had to rely on a proprietary Judd V8 engine to

The 1992 season brought Jordan and Yamaha together, and the Japanese company's V12 engine was tested in a modified 191 at the end of the previous year. It was a marriage of convenience that was not destined to last. (Formula 1 Pictures)

challenge the might of McLaren-Honda and Ferrari. It failed to win a race, but was able to reverse that in ensuing seasons when its alliance with Renault began to bear fruit.

In its own eight-year history, Jordan GP has used customer Ford V8 engines; works Yamaha V12s; customer/works Brian Hart V10s; works Peugeot V10s; and since 1998 uses works Mugen-Honda V10s. By any standard this is a chequered record, but it is more a product of circumstance than capriciousness on Jordan's behalf. In some ways the team has been a small boat tossed about on troubled seas, and its story is a modern F1 parable.

Yamaha seemed like the only game in town – Eddie lunged for it

The choice of Ford's HB V8 engine for the Jordan 191 was no choice at all, really. It was simply the best unit available to a new team. Jordan could not have hoped to attract a works engine deal at that stage, but though its HBs would generally be up to two specifications behind those used by Benetton in its works deal with Ford, in practice it would not be too much of a disadvantage at this stage of Jordan's development. Indeed, if Gary Anderson's 191 was good enough, there was every chance that car advantage might cancel out minor engine shortcoming in comparison with the Benettons. The HB was also reliable, a major plus

in a small team's favour.

So 1991 went well as far as track performance was concerned, and Team Seven Up Jordan made a strong enough impression within that maiden season to establish itself as a serious player. But it is one of the great ironies of the sport that this first year, in which Jordan showed such tremendous promise, came close to breaking it. And that 1992, which was a year of almost unmitigated disaster, helped to set the company more firmly on its feet. Such is the way in a sport in which that old adage, 'No bucks, no Buck Rogers', was never more apposite.

Although Eddie had agreed a relatively long-term arrangement with Cosworth over the supply of the HB engine, he knew well before the 1991 season had ended that there was no way he could afford to continue it. The mountain of debt saw to that. So when Yamaha's V12 engine came into the equation around the middle of 1991, the way was clear. It wasn't a great engine, and it hadn't done much for the ailing Brabham team that season, but Yamaha seemed like the only game in town, and Eddie lunged for it with all the passion of a drowning man who sees a straw floating by.

One of the author's overriding memories of the 1992 season is of walking down to the Jordan pit early one morning at Interlagos, to find that the usual pleasantries had been suspended by the toil and frustration of an endless night. The Yamaha V12 on Mauricio

New season, new look. Eddie seems preoccupied as he poses in the garb of new sponsor, Sasol. (Formula 1 Pictures)

Gugelmin's 192 had broken the previous day and been lugged out. But the moment its replacement was fitted and then fired up, that too suffered a terminal seizure.

This team has flourished while 12 others have not survived

Back in 1989 when Erich Zakowski's Zakspeed team used Yamaha's V8 engine with five-valve cylinder head technology, the team from Niederzissen in Germany had suffered similar disasters. It is said that the record for the shortness of life of an engine between start up and blow up was 54 seconds. Now, it seemed, a V12 had lowered that to 49 seconds, after several hours of work by mechanics who were plainly sick of the whole thing. As an indication of just how desperate the situation had become, there was a pan of oil literally bubbling away in one guarded corner of the tatty garage; heating the lubricant in such a Heath Robinson way offered a slim chance that the engine might live long enough at least to get the car out on to the track.

Trevor Foster rolls his eyes at such memories, in the way that both Gugelmin and Stefano Modena did in earlier years. Gugelmin, a Brazilian who had shown promise with the Leyton House team after winning the British F3 series in 1985, had switched to Jordan in 1992 with expectations of moving further up the F1 ladder; Modena was an enigmatic Italian who had shown strongly in F3 before dominating the F3000 Championship in 1987. In 1991 he had enjoyed significant reliability from Honda's heavy but dependable V10 engine while driving for Tyrrell. But now, even at this early stage of the season, at the third race, both could see their F1 careers foundering on the rock of Yamaha technology.

'The difficulty of 1992,' Foster recalls, 'was the sheer scale of the thing. It's one achievement to design and build your car in 1990, then run it in November and, with a staff of just 45 people, test and race the car right throughout 1991. But the problem is then that there were six people in the drawing office, and half of them were going to every race, as engineers.

'Now the whole timescale had to be compressed to do the same thing for the 1992 car. And up until about July or August of 1991 we still had two years of the contract to run with Ford. So the design staff were saying, "Right, we know the 1992 car is being designed around the HB engine." Then because of a combination of things – various sponsorship things not being fulfilled; because we couldn't generate the sort of money we were trying to generate in our first year; and because the costs involved were higher than we had anticipated – we were not able realistically to continue down the Ford route. The debts were there, and we just could not afford to pay the whole lease fee up front before the first race.'

To appreciate fully the dilemma facing not just Jordan, but any small

Anderson's new 192 bore a necessarily strong outward resemblance to the 191, but not for the last time the colour scheme was reworked. (LAT)

team trying to make it in the big world of F1, it's important to know the rules. Among many things, at that time these called for every team to commit to contesting all 16 World Championship rounds. In the past some teams, particularly Ferrari in the late 1960s, would take a two- or three-race sabbatical in the hope of sorting out their cars if they ran into problems, prior to what was hoped would be a competitive return. It was like a pause for breath.

But part of the push initiated by Bernie Ecclestone, towards staging a really top class show, was that everybody had to turn up for every race. There were serious cash penalties for those who failed to do so, and these, of course, had the effect not only of wors-

ening a team's financial state, but of hastening its demise. Many would cling on to the bitter end before their fingertips simply could no longer bear the weight of imminent failure, whereupon the team would drop like a stone.

In the years between Jordan's debut in 1991, and its challenge for the first victory in 1998, F1 saw the death of no fewer than 12 new teams: Fondmetal, Leyton House (which struggled on as March when Leyton House pulled out), AGS, Scuderia Italia Dallara, Larrousse Lola, Coloni, Lambo, Andrea Moda, Lola, Pacific, Simtek and Forti. And also the collapse of classic names such as Lotus and Brabham. And only fresh alliances or buyouts would save teams such as Arrows,

Ligier and Tyrrell from similar fates. Indeed, of all the teams new to F1 for the 1990s, only Jordan, Sauber and Stewart have survived thus far.

These were not comfortable statistics for a man who knew, going into 1992, that he had yet to source the sort of budget that would take him through to the end of the year. Indeed, the debts from 1991 already amounted to a worrying £4.5 million.

At the same time there was the nagging anger that money scheduled to come from deals around Michael Schumacher would now be going instead to Benetton, while the debt to Cosworth would hang round the team's neck for some time yet as legal threats ebbed and flowed in the background. All in all, it was a deeply unsettling period in the team's brief history.

'If everybody had been given a free choice, we would have stayed with Ford,' Foster avers. 'But financially we

Mauricio Gugelmin coped well with the difficult situation that Jordan encountered, and was usually the faster of its two drivers. (LAT)

had to do the Yamaha deal. There was no choice.

'The engine was free, but it wasn't just that. It was clutches, exhausts, freight, all the other bits and pieces that add up on top. And at that moment in time the only major contract we had in place for 1992 was with Barclay. Sasol would come in, of course, but right then it wasn't even a twinkle. It didn't come until the end of January 1992, and when it did it came right out of the blue. Whoosh, like that! Okay, had we known that the previous August or September, we would have stayed with Ford, because obviously if you've got fixed contracts in place, even if you haven't got the money, it gives the bank a lot more confidence.'

This was a very difficult time for Eddie Jordan himself. He had to put up all his personal properties – such as a large town house on the outskirts of Oxford, and a villa in Sotogrande, Spain – as personal guarantees against default on the Cosworth contract. That left him and his family very exposed. He could have lost everything he had ever worked for. The whole

Team-mate Stefano Modena seemed less able to shrug off the enduring disappointments, but at the end of the season he was able to score Jordan's sole point in a tough year. (LAT)

company was poised on a knife edge.

'It's all very well people saying today that Eddie is making the money, look at his life style, and all that,' Foster says defensively, 'but the risks he took in 1991 were unbelievable. He hung everything he'd worked 10 or 12 years for on the line. The luck of the Irish, skill, whatever you want to call it, that all came along. But he earned it, no question.'

The seeds of the disappointing technical year of 1992 were sown in September 1991 when Gary Anderson and his drawing office staff were informed that the Yamaha engine was replacing the Cosworth HB. The Cosworth was a compact eight cylinder unit, the Yamaha a long and relatively heavy V12. This would have to be shoehorned somehow into the 192 design which was already well advanced. Inevitably, its balance and weight distribution would thus have to be altered, so right from the start the car that the team would race in its second year would be compromised.

'Because of our limited resources we weren't really able to work that hard on the 1992 car,' Foster admits. 'And we didn't really make the step forward from the '91 car that we should have done. The '91 car was very good, but even allowing for the engine I don't think the '92 car was particularly stunning because it was all down to time and development, time in the wind tunnel . . .

On Sasol's home ground, Ivan Capelli's Jordan debut in the 193-Hart was not a happy one in the 1993 South African GP. (Formula 1 Pictures)

'We were just too exposed, stretched too thin.'

The worst part, claims Foster, was that the Yamaha V12 was a high-performance engine that had been designed with a roadcar application foremost in mind, but which had then been modified to make it suitable for F1. 'I'm not saying it was a roadcar engine as such, but it was like a high-performance roadcar power unit. It would have been like Ferrari taking its Testa Rossa engine and saying, "Listen guys, we're going to make this into an F1 engine." It just wasn't achievable.'

The V12 had been intended as the power unit of a Yamaha roadcar, penned by former McLaren and March star designer Robin Herd, which would be a rival for the McLaren F1, Ferrari F40 and Bugatti EB110 roadgoing supercars. Some cars were actually built, but the project was never successful.

'People asked us why we had worse reliability with the engine than Brabham had in 1991,' Foster said, 'and we'd answer that Yamaha was trying to stretch it to another level. Yamaha had to rev it higher to get more power and the engine just wasn't designed around that ethos. It was totally out of the ballpark for what it was meant to be. And from that it generated all sorts of problems. It generated too much heat, and they got themselves into real trouble because they changed all the specification, and they couldn't go back to the original because the cylinder heads were different. They were really verging out of control and it was very haphazard. Engines were coming left, right and centre with different specifications, because they were trying to move forward.

'We were the first team to use a sequential gearbox, and that in itself broke some new ground but prompted problems in its own right. So there was all this going on in the background, and we were just for ever fighting, trying to dig ourselves out of holes. I mean, we had some engines seize up while the cars were on stands, as they did in Brazil. We had them blowing up going out of the pits. In South Africa we blew three engines. We stood there in final qualifying on Saturday afternoon, we didn't have one car in the garage. One had blown out on the circuit, one of them even blew up going out of the pit lane. In Mexico one seized its bearings and the other, Stefano's, blew up going on to the grid so he had to take the spare car. That was the way it was.

'The whole thing was bordering out of control, and you couldn't get it back into control. People suggested we'd under-estimated the cooling capacity of the V12 engine. Well, with the Cosworth engine we were given the cooling parameters and we never had to change anything on the car. With the Yamaha we were putting more cooling ducts in the bodywork and still the thing was a teapot!'

Gugelmin and his wife Stella grimace at the lap times as they watch his F1 career slipping away. Engineer Andy Green can't bear to look. (Formula 1 Pictures)

The life of Brian: working with Brian Hart

If Eddie Jordan is the last great privateer among modern F1 team owners, then Brian Hart is his counterpart in the engine stakes. Somehow their respective statuses made their two-year alliance all the more apposite.

Working without fanfare from premises in Harlow, Essex, Hart raised the £2 million needed to develop his 10.35 V10 F1 engine and just got on with the job in typically no-nonsense manner. Not for him the ballyhoo of corporate marketing. When you meet this former racer, whose looks belie his 60-plus years, what you see is precisely what you get. A shrewd, honest engineer who knows how to make engines work – 'Jam Tart' loves them. To witness the familiar bronzed bald head bent over one of his units at a race is to witness one of the sport's more straightforward racers doing what he loves best.

Hart's own racing career took him as high as Formula 2, where he acquitted himself well against drivers who had successful Grand Prix careers. When he hung up his helmet, his engines carried on winning races, and one of the highlights was Mike Hailwood's European F2 Championship success with a Surtees-Hart in 1972.

Everyone who used his engines knew that if they returned them in a dirty condition for a rebuild, they would not be touched. Hart expects customers to treat his products with due respect. When he supplied the Footwork team in 1996, driver Jos Verstappen's manager, former F2 racer Huub Rothengatter, found himself on the receiving end of some uncompromising – and uncharacteristic – Hart invective on one occasion when he forgot that.

Hart likes to work in his own way, with a handful of trusted aides. You sense that he enjoys the David and Goliath nature of his fight against the major manufacturers. All of them respect his ability and his engines, and the sort of independent pride that saw him buy himself back out of Cosworth ownership a while ago. It did not go unnoticed in 1994 that his V10 was holding its end up nobly against Peugeot's significantly better funded unit, which at one stage showed a remarkable appetite for explosive self-destruction.

Hart is not a great man for meetings or committees. In that he has much in common with Eddie Jordan and Gary Anderson. And, like them, he could turn round new components very quickly if the necessity arose. 'I suppose one thing that we have, and it's completely obvious, is response,' he says in his customarily quiet manner. 'If I go back on Sunday night, I can have faxes and it's happening on Monday morning. I presume Renault can do that, but it's got to go through a certain process of engineers and decision making, and maybe even cost. But I can just decide, "Bang! Do it!" I think that just because we're small doesn't necessarily mean it's a hindrance.'

Over the course of 1993 he would gradually allow the Jordan drivers a handful more revs here and there, depending on his development schedule, and like Jordan himself he understood that when finance is not boundless, a wise man has to know, and operate within, his limitations.

Though Hart is the last person to broadcast it, John Barnard was interested in the engine while working on what would become a stillborn F1 project, and again when he went back to Ferrari. Meanwhile the Jordan decision literally beat a prevaricating Ron Dennis of McLaren by a matter of hours. Hart grins at the latter recollection. 'The only people that we hadn't talked to, direct, were McLaren, funnily enough. The information we had is that they were almost certainly going to attempt to do a deal for Ligier's Renault engines, or with Ford. Then we received a call from Ron, and I told him we'd done a deal with Eddie. It was one of those things.'

Brian Hart has come a long, long way on the sort of budget that wouldn't keep even the publicity machines of Renault, Peugeot or Honda lubricated for a season. Up to the point of going racing with Sasol Jordan, he had probably spent very little more than £2 million. Small beer to a grandee, a vast sum of your own money.

He's disarmingly modest when asked to quantify the attributes behind his engine's creation. 'There were a lot of small things. There was no one major thing. Part of it is having a reasonable understanding of the priorities. Like, it has to cool and it has to be pretty reliable, otherwise you can't improve the car. You can't try and make the engine work at the track. When it arrives here it's like a set of tyres. You just put them in and take them out. Though we weren't funded enough, we did have the benefit of several months of r&d without the pressure of going racing as well. And I think that had quite a bit to do with it.'

At the time of going to press, the closest a Hart engine has come to winning a Grand Prix was Monaco in 1984. Ayrton Senna's brilliantly-driven turbo Toleman was hacking into Alain Prost's advantage when the wet race was stopped prematurely. But Hart has never stopped trying ever since.

At the 1994 Belgian GP, powered by the Hart V10, Barrichello made the best use of varying weather conditions in practice to snatch his, and Jordan's, first F1 pole position. (LAT)

All of this extra ducting and radiator area increased drag, which in turn increased fuel consumption, which demanded greater fuel load and added to the car's overall weight. Which required greater power, which generated more heat. And so it went on. It was a vicious circle, with no escape. In 1991 it had taken Jordan Grand Prix only five races to score its first World Championship points; in 1992 the team had an agonising wait until the final round in Australia before Modena dragged his car home in sixth place to score one point.

Foster recalled: 'From having cars that were on the weight limit, in 1991, we were fighting to keep the cars within 10 kilos of the weight limit. And once you get into something like that, it's really, really difficult to pull yourself out of it.'

Yamaha of course saw the situation rather differently, maintaining faith with the engine and suggesting that the root of the problem lay within its installation in the Jordan. The relationship was often strained.

Formula 1 engine deals are a technological marriage, and there are always two sides in any divorce. 'I don't really think that the engine was as bad as painted,' a Yamaha spokesman told the

Instead, the star in the camp in 1993 was the upcoming young Brazilian, Rubens Barrichello, who impressed frequently. (LAT)

author in 1998. 'And it was always intended as an F1 engine; it wasn't just derived from a roadgoing sportscar power unit. It's important to remember that it did well with the Brabham team in 1991, when it scored World Championship points.

'Our feeling at Yamaha during 1992 was certainly that it was never cooled properly throughout the year. That was the major problem, and it was not our responsibility. Perhaps going from a proprietary V8 engine to a factory V12 was a bit more difficult than Jordan had envisaged.

Returning to the privateer route for engines was a brave move

---

'I'm not saying the engine was perfect. It had a detonation problem for much of the season, which we felt was down to the fuel. That reached a peak around Imola. But overall the Yamaha V12 wasn't as bad as it was sometimes claimed to be.'

Foster says: 'The only thing it did do was help us to get back on to a bit more of a sound financial footing. So although it wasn't a success on the track, from a company point of view it gave us the funding to be able to survive.'

The team couldn't pay off all the debts, but there was enough to keep creditors away. Eddie Jordan came to arrangements so that they were paid, and eventually in later years a settle-ment would also be reached to sort out the debt with Cosworth. But by the end of the 1992 season everyone breathed a collective sigh of relief as the agreement with Yamaha ended, and the Japanese company went on to a more promising relationship with Tyrrell using an engine based on a V10 designed by John Judd's Engine Developments company in Rugby.

Jordan, meanwhile, turned to a similar configuration powerplant after a series of talks with builder Brian Hart of Harlow, Essex. It would seem like manna from heaven.

Hart had begun to examine the feasibility of his new engine late in 1991, just as Jordan was counting its debt. 'In actual fact it started off as a V8 for a variety of reasons. Then I went to a couple of races and completely reappraised my thoughts. Long-term, given all the stability that we thought we had, there would be more potential, as I saw it, in a V10. You have to remember how the fuel regulations were then, too, things like that. So we decided on a 10. We laid down three prototypes and ran those continuously from very early 1992 onwards.'

He did the design work himself, as usual, with the assistance of friend and employee John Lievesley. It took about five months to complete the full concept, design and drawing. And as soon as possible all of the major components, such as crankshafts which have the longest lead items, were put in hand. Lievesley concen-trated on the camshafts and valve gear, while Hart focused on the general layout and the structures.

Underlining the commitment necessary to compete at the top level of the sport, the 28-strong Jordan race team poses in Adelaide at the end of 1993. (Formula 1 Pictures)

'During 1992 we were faced with a bit of a dilemma. Should we plough in the remaining money that we had – because we weren't with a team then but financing everything ourselves. But it was a matter of biting the bullet, as this was the only way we could carry the company forward. So we just went for it with our own engine.

'Having made that decision we then had to make another: How long do we carry on doing the initial work? The actual cost of getting to a prototype engine is fairly calculable. You know how long people are going to work on the drawings, you know how much the patterns are going to cost, you know how much the castings are going to be. The bit that then costs a lot of money is running it on the dynamometer, and finding what you need to change.'

He went to the San Marino Grand Prix at Imola in 1992, to test the water and try to ascertain likely demand for a new engine, and via Trevor Foster and Gary Anderson he talked with Yamaha. 'It wasn't really anything more perhaps than some joint effort to help look at the V12. But it didn't work out. We got very close to coming to an agreement to do something with them but we decided not to.'

Instead he continued to talk with other teams. 'I went along to the pre-Grand Prix test at Silverstone, got to talk to Gary again, and by this stage it was fair to say that they were wondering what they were going to have to do, or where to go. So after the Grand Prix he said, "Well, what about your engine, then?" That was the first time he or Trevor had mentioned my engine. So I said, "Come down and have a look." They came down, we showed them the prototypes, how many hours we'd been running. We talked in great detail. All the basics. Weight, size, length, what we thought it would cool. So then Gary said, "Well I'd like to do a proposal to Eddie."'

As the 1992 situation with Yamaha grew ever less tolerable, Foster and Anderson had lobbied Jordan hard about the potential of Hart's neat but under-funded engine. 'We couldn't see any major progress being made on the Yamaha front by mid-season,' Foster

No respecter of reputations, Eddie Irvine rekindled his relationship with Jordan as he swept dramatically into F1 at the end of 1993, and impressed sufficiently to secure the seat for 1994. (LAT)

recalled, 'and for 1993 we needed to look to an alternative source. The problem was that obviously Eddie still wasn't out of the financial wood.

'I'd known Brian for years because I met him when he was still driving in F2 himself, so we'd often chatted in the paddock. Now he told us that he'd got this V10 engine of his own, and had built a couple of prototypes. Gary and I went down to have a look at it, and we talked to Eddie about it. And Eddie said well, yes, whatever. But to be honest about it, having stretched himself out right across the wire, he was obviously going to be very reluctant to admit to having to go back and pay for an engine. And that was the bottom line with Brian. So that was obviously a major thing to him.

'We'd gone through the various

discussions; we'd tried to get Brian involved with Yamaha's problems; we'd tried to get Yamaha to badge Brian's engine. But at the end of the day I think Brian was not prepared to move beyond a certain level and basically told them that their V12 was nowhere near suitable for F1. There was no way it could be modified, they really needed to start again from scratch.'

'The proposal went to Eddie in early August, and the problem was that it was now getting very tight to get the engine built,' Hart recalled. 'And the regulation changes meant that it would almost have to be in a hybrid V12 chassis, which isn't what Gary or I wanted but we really didn't have a choice.

'Then from Monza the deal was all done by telephone and fax, and in mid-October we signed a deal for two years exclusive, which we both thought was very important. It had to be a 100 per cent effort with one team.'

Foster resumed: 'I think it was right up until September before the decision to go with Brian was made and Eddie finally conceded and said, "Okay guys, get Brian here. Let's do the deal." But once again, that was a fairly brave thing for Eddie to do, to give up that little bit of financial comfort that had been there with Yamaha, and to go again down the privateer route.'

It was the perfect solution to the short-term problems, but again there

Irvine's first race for Jordan in 1994, in Brazil, was a troubled affair that led to a three-race suspension being imposed by the sport's governing body. (LAT)

was a knock-on effect which reveals just how critical engine supply stability is in F1.

'I think '93 really was the same as '92,' Foster suggests. 'Yes, we had a better engine, but we still had very restricted technical resources. And having spent the whole year fighting fires with the engine and trying to get the engine running and the car going better in 1992, not enough time could be allocated to producing a better car in 1993.

Jordan now had engine continuity plus competitive team-mates

'Brian's engine in comparison with the Yamaha was a joy to work with, and ran and ran. He did a fantastic job and it performed really well, and Gary and Brian obviously hit it off straight away on a working level. But there were some shortcomings in the car that weren't fully appreciated until quite late in the year, because of lack of time and resources such as the man-hours to get into the car and find out what they were.'

Jordan was also still a relatively inexperienced team, and in the upcoming young Brazilian Rubens Barrichello it had a driver who was in his first F1 car and therefore could not be expected to draw any serious comparison with anything he had driven previously at that level. It would not be until the 1993 Italian GP at Monza that

September that an underrated Italian called Marco Apicella would help to put his finger on a handling problem. Veteran of countless F3000 races, and seen by some as one of the talents that got away, Apicella advised that the 193 needed a longer wheelbase, and in such guise it began to pick up pace again at the end of the year.

At the same time the insouciant Ulsterman Eddie Irvine had bounced into F1 alongside Barrichello at the Japanese GP at Suzuka, where Barrichello finished fifth and he was sixth. Not everyone cared for Irvine's apparent take-it-or-leave-it indifference to F1. He enraged Ayrton Senna sufficiently during and immediately after the race for the Brazilian to throw a clumsy punch at him in the team's cabin, after Senna had won and Irvine had fought hard for some World Championship points on his debut.

But the second Eddie played one key role, and that was to get Barrichello all fired up again after he had fallen into rather too comfortable a routine as the team's darling. Now Jordan for the first time had two team-mates who would provide strong feedback while also really pushing one another along, strong factors in any car's development.

The other vital element was that for the first time in its existence Jordan Grand Prix would go into a new season with the same engine it had run in the previous year. This gave Anderson some crucial continuity as he drew out the 194 for the 1994 season. The importance of this could not be understated within the factory. As a result the 194 was a very good little car that

This shot, taken in Spain 1994, captures the relationship between Irvine and Barrichello, who were uneasy bedfellows at the best of times. (Formula 1 Pictures)

performed well throughout the year, one highlight coming when, via a series of circumstances centred on Spa's very unpredictable weather, Barrichello found himself on pole position for the Belgian GP after setting his best qualifying lap at precisely the right moment.

There were lows as well, however. At Imola, during the fateful meeting in which Roland Ratzenberger and Ayrton Senna would be killed, Barrichello was extremely lucky to survive after his Jordan crashed spectacularly at the Traguardo corner during practice. He was only saved by very quick medical intervention. Prior to that, Irvine had been involved in an accident at the first race in Brazil, for which he was suspended for one race; when Jordan appealed to the FIA

against the severity of the penalty, it found out the hard way that nobody wins against the sport's governing body – the ban was increased threefold.

But once again the team was moving forward. It had finished joint eleventh (and last) in the 1992 Constructors' Championship with one point. In 1993 it was still bottom of the league but had three points; now it was up to fifth with a very respectable 28 points. That was where it had finished in 1991, but now it had more than twice as many points and had seen its first podium finish. Barrichello had finished fourth in Brazil, then third at Aida before his Imola shunt, and then recovered to take fourths in Britain, Italy, Portugal and Australia. Meanwhile, good old Andrea de Cesaris stood in for Irvine at Imola and then Monaco, where he boosted morale by finishing a steady fourth. Once he recovered his momentum, Irvine took sixth in the Spanish GP at Barcelona, fourth in the GP of Europe at Jerez, and fifth at Suzuka.

'All of this,' Foster summarised, 'gave Jordan the credentials to be approached by Peugeot for 1995.' The team was on the brink of another big sea change.

To be taken seriously you need the clout of a manufacturer

It was a shame that the Hart deal had to come to an end, says commercial director Ian Phillips. 'It did work extremely well. We paid him on the dot, every month. I think that the two years we were together, we were a day late once with our payment. And I think that Brian would say that we were the best people as far as payment was concerned. It was a good deal. But the problem is such an engine is a bloody difficult thing to sell. You need the clout of a manufacturer. You really do.

'At the end of the day engines are about one man. Ilmor is about Mario Illien. Yes, there are a whole load of back-up staff, but the brilliant guys are the ones who design the engines, like Paul Rosche at BMW, Bernard Dudot when he was at Renault, Jean-Pierre Boudy at Peugeot. And Brian was that man. Perhaps in the long run we should have set up our own engine company. But you have to have the

clout of a manufacturer to be taken seriously, I suppose. It's difficult to say how much further we could have gone with Brian. Obviously he needed further investment, and the money to make that investment, without a manufacturer's name attached to it, is difficult to find. We tried attracting a manufacturer in to buy it . . .'

This was Austin Rover. Back in early 1993 the team mocked up an engine and car with apposite livery and logos, and made a presentation to ARG personnel at the Jordan factory. But though there was a level of interest, the company didn't bite.

'It's a very, very cheap way into F1,' Phillips insists. '£3 million, it was then. And you can hardly buy signage on a car today for that sort of money. We just wanted to cover our costs. That's what we were looking for at the time. But it was an incredibly cheap way in, even if you had turned round to somebody and said it was £5 million but you don't have to lift a finger. It's there! Just badge the cam covers and away you go.'

Back in 1966 Walter Hayes at Ford Motor Company sanctioned the investment of £100,000 – at that time a significant sum – in the development of the V8 engine that was to be designed by Keith Duckworth at Cosworth Engineering. Badged as a Ford it went on not just to win its debut race, when Jim Clark's Lotus 49

After a strong start to the 1994 season Barrichello dipped a little before recovering momentum in the second half. Here manager Geraldo Rodrigues helps him to prepare for battle in Hungary. (Formula 1 Pictures)

triumphed in the 1967 Dutch GP at Zandvoort, but to take another 154 victories over the next 16 years and establish itself as the most successful F1 powerplant of all time. It was an amazing return on the investment. But in the money-conscious days of the early 1990s men with Hayes' brand of corporate courage were thin on the ground. Hart himself would try hard with the emergent Daewoo company, but met with a similar lack of success on that front.

From the start it was clear that the Peugeot deal was doomed

Hart was quite comfortable with the idea of a major manufacturer badging his engine. 'We have had an approach. It would be improper to say who.' (He is not referring to Rover. Jordan's 1993 overture was made at a time when Rover's financial resources were too stretched even though its technical staff were very keen. Many think that the company to which Hart alluded was Daewoo.)

'We agreed that Jordan could co-seek engineering back-up finance for the engine, leading up to badging it, which we were quite happy to do provided the terms were agreeable. I think it's probably fair to say though that the recession killed off any chance of it happening. But we are still actively looking for more engineering finance.' Hart would have no problem

cementing the sort of deal that Ford enjoys with Cosworth, rather than just assisting a manufacturer. The Yamaha situation, for example, was more a direct consultancy on research and development, whereas he would far prefer to be hands on.

Though Jordan is once again past such concerns, Phillips still remains convinced that they have serious merit. 'It's is a very cheap way in and I still believe that there is potential for those sort of deals. At the end of the day Ford has to go to Cosworth, Mercedes goes to Ilmor. Why shouldn't Daewoo go to Brian Hart, if that is what it requires? Because a small specialist can do the job. If we could have done that, I think we would have been very happy.

'We tried over a period of two years, and through Brian we got ourselves into a pretty lucky position. We had a Ford contract and a Peugeot contract to examine. The thing is it had taken Ford four months to get a contract to us; it took Peugeot about seven days. And at the end of the day the Peugeot one might have been short-termish, and they wanted it to happen. Ford only wanted it to happen when it was too late. They'd been busy entertaining offers from all over the place.'

Peugeot had decided to emulate rival Renault by entering F1 in 1994, and did so with the McLaren team. But to outsiders it seemed a frosty and uncomfortable relationship born of necessity for both parties. McLaren had been the super-dominant team of the mid to late 1980s, winning 12 of the 16 races in 1984 and 15 in 1988. But since losing Honda engines at the

New power and new hopes characterised the team's 1995 offensive, as Peugeot threw its V10 weight behind Anderson's new design. The garish blue, red and yellow colour scheme had mercifully disappeared by the time the racing season started. (Formula 1 Pictures)

end of 1992 the team had endured a season as a quasi-customer of Ford in 1993. Though it had won five races courtesy of Senna, who left to drive for Williams at the end of the season, it too desperately sought a works engine deal and Peugeot appeared to be the only party which fitted the bill.

The problem was that McLaren wanted an engine that could win races, and the Peugeot wasn't ready for that, although Martin Brundle did finish second at Monaco and Mika Hakkinen was similarly placed in Belgium. When McLaren agreed terms with Mercedes-Benz for 1995, Peugeot suddenly needed a new partner and Jordan seemed perfectly cast in the role.

'Obviously Peugeot had had a pretty steep learning curve with McLaren,'

Foster surmised, 'and yet again as late as September time Gary and his lads were told, "Hang on guys, it's the Peugeot V10 not the Hart for the new car". Again there was this huge turn of direction. That's fine in so far as the engine comes as a package with radiators and so on and was built by a major manufacturer, but it still needed to be supported by the Jordan side.' And at that time the Jordan team was still cutting its teeth and going through growing pains. The workforce had now grown to around 60 people, but this was far short of what was needed to cope with sudden changes of direction.

The ensuing three seasons saw Jordan Grand Prix maturing further, without ever quite making it home first. 1995 brought second place for

Barrichello in Canada, where Irvine backed him with third place, fourth for Barrichello at the Nurburgring and for Irvine in Japan, fifth for Irvine in Spain, sixth for Barrichello in France and Belgium and for Irvine at the Nurburgring. This placed the team sixth in the Constructors' Championship with 21 points, but it was a disappointment.

Things weren't much better in 1996. With the cars painted for the first time in the gold of new sponsor Benson & Hedges, much was expected, but the headlines that Martin Brundle made on his return to the team for the first time since his F3 days centred on his escape from a spectacular crash in the first race of the season, in Melbourne.

The 196 lacked downforce in comparison with its rivals, and though the team again took fifth place in the Constructors' Championship (22 points), it was a disappointing year with the usual lower top six placings for both Brundle and Barrichello.

The 1997 season would be better, with the 197 registering a marked improvement and, as we shall see later, the team coming close to its first victory. But right from the start it was clear that the alliance with Peugeot was doomed. Jordan had foreseen that however and opened talks with the Japanese Mugen-Honda company. This meant yet another change of engine manufacturer, but this time it was one that Jordan knew very well from the successful F3000 alliance which had seen Jean Alesi winning the 1989 European F3000 Championship with Mugen power.

The writing had long been on the wall with Peugeot, from the moment that Alain Prost purchased the Ligier team and France suddenly again dared to envisage the chauvinistic dream of blue cars with French engines, chassis, drivers and tyres. This time Jordan had been talking to Mugen-Honda since 1996, and the situation was thus very well advanced.

'Of course we were aware that the

renewal with Peugeot was coming round,' Foster says, 'and we couldn't get any firm indication about the Prost thing or from Peugeot, so you have to go your own route and be ready for something else so the company can survive and go motor racing. And of the various options that were available to us, we decided that Mugen-Honda was the best one for us. It was all less of a problem because by then we had more equipment and more people and facilities.

'We didn't want to launch the 198 any earlier than we had the 197 or the 196; basically what it means is that your build time can be shorter and your design time therefore can be longer. You never achieve perfection, but while you're looking for it you are always improving your basic product. With a better timescale you can get people looking far deeper into the various areas of the car, and the understanding of an F1 car for us is probably 10 times more now than what it was three years ago.'

That understanding was only truly reflected in 1997, by which time Jordan's technological level was dramatically different. But to get there had taken some serious funding.

Chapter 4

Where does all the money come from?

Survival in F1 calls for an innate ability to juggle – and generate – huge levels of finance. It's multi-million dollar stuff, easy to spend when you have it, frighteningly difficult to find when you don't. And not a job for the faint-hearted. In 1997, for example, Williams's operating budget was believed to be £20 million; McLaren's was estimated to be 50 per cent higher still. And such sums are often matched by the engine supplier. Nobody knows just how much Ferrari, the only team which still manufactures its own engines, spends.

On the face of it, a change of engine supplier naturally affects the technical department far more than any other, but there are inevitably knock-on effects elsewhere in an F1 team. 'You've got to re-livery everything,' Ian Phillips says. 'You've got to throw away tens of thousands of pounds' worth of clothing and print work, stuff like that, though I suppose we tend to throw it away every year anyway. But it's a shame for all that, because it's one of the wasteful areas. But without it we can't exist, so everybody has got to have their corporate identity, and that's the way it is. It's just something that takes up a lot of time.'

But in his role as commercial director Phillips was ideally placed to see that the change from Hart to Peugeot engines for 1995 cut deeper than that and levied its own unexpected toll on Jordan Grand Prix's financial situation. He is closely involved with such negotiations, since invariably there are not just technical aspects but marketing considerations too.

'I got very involved with the Mugen-Honda deal, in that Eddie and I went to all the initial talks, starting at Suzuka in 1996. We approached them, which wasn't difficult because of the

Man with a Mission. One of Eddie Jordan's greatest assets is his wide circle of acquaintances in the racing paddocks of the world. (LAT)

Here he converses with Ian Phillips, one of his right-hand men at Jordan Grand Prix who takes the role of commercial director. (LAT)

strong past relationship. We had one preliminary meeting, then met with Hirotoshi Honda himself and took it from there.'

Seeing the future is part of the trick to surviving in F1. Eddie Jordan already felt that the relationship with Peugeot was unlikely to last. Looking for alternatives at an early stage was pure commonsense.

'It was fairly obviously that Peugeot didn't really want us,' Phillips claims. 'There was no real passion. They didn't seem to understand – and it was probably what prevented us from making the deal work – that Jordan had to generate funding. And we were very honest with them from day one; we weren't McLaren. It wasn't open cheque book racing.'

In retrospect it would probably have been better for both parties if Peugeot had started with Jordan, rather than with McLaren. Instead, in its first F1 season the French company found itself with a team that expected victory; in its second, with one that lacked the serious funding of its predecessor. This was a difficult predicament for all concerned.

'In the first year we had really nothing,' Phillips suggests, when describing Jordan's financial state. 'But we did our best. The second year we got Benson & Hedges in, and Peugeot almost tried to

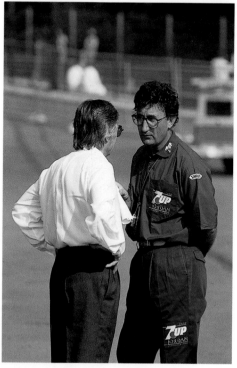

Jordan is also close to F1's ultimate powerbroker, Bernie Ecclestone. (LAT)

Frank Williams, who has set standards of excellence and success to which all F1 team owners aspire, listens as Jordan makes a point. (LAT)

stop us from doing that! They told us that we couldn't have a gold car. Nobody really knows why, but obstacles were put in our way all the time.

'In 1995 Peugeot owned an awful lot of space on the car. They owned the Total space, for which Total put $12 million in Peugeot's coffers and we received not one penny. We wanted the rear wing back because it was the only way we could extend the deal with Benson & Hedges for 1997, but to

This time it's Peter Sauber and Jean Todt of Ferrari receiving the wisdom, in the old upper paddock at the Hungaroring. (LAT)

Golden chance: signing with Benson & Hedges

There was a degree of good fortune involved when Jordan Grand Prix met and courted the Benson & Hedges tobacco brand, and then tied the knot with almost indecent haste early in the 1996 season. But in motor racing as in any other walk of life, the luck you enjoy is very often the luck you have made for yourself. Commercial director Ian Phillips and his team had been keeping a close eye on the tobacco situation, and one of its forays into the market coincided with the right circumstances and resulted in a successful proposal. Like many really good deals, it all came together very quickly. Phillips metaphorically rubs his hands together at the memory, not just because of the sums involved, you suspect, but because of the sheer thrill of the chase.

'We heard a whisper the week before Christmas in 1995, that the ownership of the brand had been sorted out. So we pursued it. We had a preliminary meeting on 6 January, and signed the deal on the 14th, I think it was.

'We hadn't been into Gallahers since we'd seen them about Silk Cut at the end of 1991. Eddie and I did one presentation at the factory, to Benson & Hedges. It was that under-rehearsed that we looked at each other and said, "Who's going to do this?" And we did it to marketing director Nigel Northridge, who is a good bloke, and to marketing manager Barry Jenner. And

about half an hour after they'd left, as they were driving home, they phoned up and said could we go and give the same presentation to the chairman at Weybridge, about four days later? So we did, and two days after that Eddie and I went down there and shook hands on the deal. Then it was a case of all hands on the gold spray paint! By that time we were about a month from the team having to leave for the first race . . .'

The paint was barely dry on some of the equipment when it was unpacked in Melbourne for the Australian GP at Albert Park early in March, and such was the haste that the cars were painted a nasty mustardy yellow in an attempt to ensure

that they would stand out on television and in black and white photographs. Later, when Ian Hutchinson had had the necessary time to research more, the paintwork changed to a stunning dual-gold colour which instantly became one of the all-time classic sponsor liveries.

In the Benson & Hedges alliance everybody at Jordan could sense the chance at last to allow the team to grow and to invest sufficiently to get up with the sport's established top four teams – Williams, McLaren, Ferrari and Benetton. It was an answer to prayers.

For their part, B&H were happy too. Half way through his company's first season with Jordan, Benson & Hedges marketing director Nigel Northridge knew they had made the right decision.

'It's clearly the most expensive of all the sponsorships we are involved in, but to a large extent you get what you pay for. In terms of trying to build a brand's exposure across Europe, the number of hours of television exposure that you can get from Formula 1 beats every other sponsorship. F1 is quite clearly at the top, and Jordan is just a great team to be with.'

The early mustard yellow soon gave way to tasteful dual-gold, creating a classic sponsorship livery that rivalled the Seven Up deal of 1991. (LAT)

No man dares be an F1 island. Jean Alesi regards his old boss as Arrows chief Tom Walkinshaw hears Eejay out. (Formula 1 Pictures)

get that we had to pay Peugeot £3 million. I suppose effectively it was only a semi-works engine deal; nothing is for free. And in some ways it would actually have been easier to pay for engines after all! That way we could have had that three million and offered it to Damon for 1997.'

The approach for Hill's services – when it became apparent in the middle of his 1996 World Championship bid that Williams would be releasing him – was another indication of Jordan's determination to up its game. But Hill preferred what he saw and heard at Arrows, when Tom Walkinshaw took him round the opulent headquarters at Leafield. Although Jordan's people took a resigned view of the loss, the rest of the world saw it as a snub: that Hill's decision suggested Jordan simply

didn't have what it took.

Phillips, predictably, gives a different view. 'When we didn't get Damon it was essentially a financial thing. If we had been able to say yes on day one, bang, I'm sure we'd have got his attention. But we had to build ourselves up from a position to be able to scrape together two million, to offering I think it was five million, in dollars. Peugeot was taking three million in pounds off us, and there were occasions when Peugeot could have helped to try and allow us to have the facilities to do the job. But they never once showed any inclination to do so. And there was all sorts of posturing going on. They never told us about Prost; we just read it in the press.'

Alain Prost wanted to change the Ligier team's name to his own when he

Such strong relationships frequently bear fruit. In late 1995 Jordan 'sold' Eddie Irvine on to Ferrari, where Todt wanted him as Michael Schumacher's partner. Jordan, Irvine and Todt celebrate at the new Nurburgring. (ICN UK Bureau)

acquired the team for the 1997 season. Under the terms of the Concorde Agreement, the document by which F1 is governed, he had to obtain permission for the change from each of his fellow team owners. When he did the rounds seeking such mandates the sticking point was Jordan, and Eddie was immediately perceived to be holding out for a windfall pound of flesh. The background details lend a fresh perspective to the situation, however, especially as it was obvious to Jordan all along that Peugeot would be headed back across the Channel at the earliest opportunity. The team was duly paid an 'inconvenience fee' (though not necessarily by Peugeot or Prost), and it all helped. Such are the workings of F1.

The alliance with Peugeot was thus an uneasy one, and it got worse after former Renault F1 racer Jean-Pierre Jabouille was replaced as overall co-ordinator. Phillips says: 'It was never a smooth relationship at all. After Jabouille left there was no passion at all. It was being run by businessmen who, to us, didn't seem to understand. With works engines you expect updates and all the rest of it. Everybody got pretty frustrated.

Peugeot firmly refutes suggestions that it was not fully committed to the cause, and maintained in an interview with the author in 1998 that its engine was capable of victory in the right circumstances. As with the Yamaha situation, every story has two sides, but there is nothing like the heat of Formula 1 battle – and disappointment

It's not all serious business in F1. Eddie indulges his passion for music . . . (LAT)

. . . as Eddie Irvine, Johnny Herbert and David Coulthard provide the vocals at the post-British GP gig organised annually by Jordan. (ICN UK Bureau)

Happy Birthday, and at the Brazilian GP in March 1996 Eddie Jordan doesn't look a day over 48. (Formula 1 Pictures)

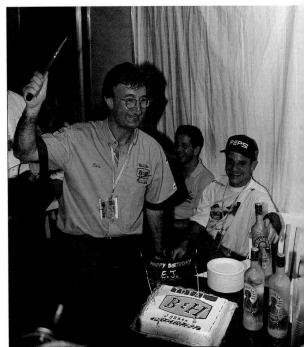

– to show up a relationship's weak points. Had the two parties been winning from the outset, their views would doubtless have been different.

I remember him all the time telling us how good he was going to be

'All that being said,' Phillips continued, 'it wasn't a bad engine.' Indeed, after Hill had expressed his surprise at the speed of the Jordans on the straights at Spa-Francorchamps during the 1996 Belgian GP, a tide of opinion began to spread that the Peugeot was a match for the Renault V10, which was the established yardstick. In 1997 it was reckoned to be close to the Mercedes-Benz V10 in the ultimate power stakes. When the Italian driver Jarno Trulli first tried the unit in a 1998 Prost AP01 – in comparison ironically enough with the Mugen-Honda V10 which powered the car the previous season and had now gone to Jordan – he said: 'I'm very impressed with the engine's smoothness, and with its top-end power.'

But Phillips remains unimpressed by Jordan's experience of the engine. 'It was good, but it was nowhere near as good as everybody tried to make out. Just because a car is quick in a straight line doesn't necessarily mean the engine is good; it means that you're not carrying enough downforce! Which certainly in 1996 was our case. And possibly again to an extent in 1997.

The Peugeot was not the all-singing, all-dancing engine, and if Alain Prost thought that was the case he was in for a very rude shock. Anyway, it was fairly obvious that Peugeot wasn't going to be a long-term option at all.'

Phillips began his career as a journalist. He's one of those enduring fellows in the sport who have paid their dues. The day he learned that he had been made editor of the highly influential weekly magazine *Autosport*, was the day he heard that his very close friend Roger Williamson had been killed in the 1973 Dutch GP at Zandvoort. Later he moved on to help Williamson's mentor, Leicestershire developer Tom Wheatcroft, run Donington Park before another spell of journalism presaged a move to run March's F3000 and then F1 efforts, under the aegis of wealthy Japanese sponsor Leyton House. In 1990 he contracted viral meningitis during the weekend of the Brazilian GP, and when he had recovered several months later it was to find that the people then operating the team had decided to dispense with his services.

Best known initially for F3 and then F2 race reporting for *Autosport*, Phillips also contributed seasonal reviews to the *Autocourse* annual. Here's what he said about Eddie Jordan in 1979, when they were on opposite sides of the F3 fence: 'Nobody really expected too much from Eddie Jordan but the man has belief in himself, and towards the end of the year fully justified himself with some strong drives.' Phillips roars with laughter when reminded of his words.

He is a typical F1 cynic in many

senses. But there is strong pride under the veneer and it surfaces as he recounts that he was the thirty-ninth person to join Jordan Grand Prix. 'I guess Eddie approached me the day after I got the sack at Leyton House. I think I got sacked on Monday and did the deal with Eddie on the Friday, something like that.' He has trouble recalling precisely when they first met, beyond it being 'sometime in the 1970s when Eejay was racing. But I suspect it was when he was visiting a hostelry in London known as The Windsor Castle. The office was in Piccadilly, Regent House, by the tube station. Everybody knew that if you wanted your name in the paper in those days you had to go to The Windsor Castle, and I have the feeling that's where I first met him properly. It sort of moved on from there.

'I saw him racing Atlantic, and probably saw him a lot when he was racing at Donington because the Irish contingent often took a weekend on the mainland. I remember him coming to my house with my old mate Chris Witty one day, and him sitting there just talking, telling us all the time about how good he was going to be.'

Phillips, like Jordan, Gary Anderson and Trevor Foster, remains unchanged by the years and by his role in F1. His

Warm embrace for the goodies

The precise breakdown of pure money in F1 has long been one of its most jealously guarded secrets, and nobody outside the fraternity is privy to the exact value of a victory, podium finish or pole position for example. But teams do of course earn well from their success on the track.

Since 1997 they have also been granted by the FIA a significantly larger chunk of the copious revenue from television. This is calculated on an ad hoc basis taking into account factors such as the length of time that a team has been contesting the championship, its level of success, and the air time that its cars win. At the same time it earns additional revenue from licensing agreements around the world which take the form of rights to scale models manufactured by corporate third parties, and/or rights and sales of official merchandising such as team jackets and caps.

In 1997 Giancarlo Minardi, founder of the Minardi team, welcomed the new proportion of television income. 'It is as if we have done a deal with a sponsor who does not want any identity on the car, leaving us free to sell it to someone else.'

Certainly the new avenues of income helped teams to operate on a much more stable basis, but the trick as always for the newcomers was to survive. Having got this far, Jordan found the new source a godsend. It was thus hardly surprising that while better established teams such as Williams, McLaren and Tyrrell stood firm and refused to agree the terms of the new Concorde Agreement, the sport's governing document by which (among other things) the share of such goodies was liberated, Eddie Jordan embraced it warmly.

job as commercial director is to generate revenue streams, and this comes obviously from commercial sponsorship, but also from less highlighted activities, such as licensing agreements. It's high-pressure stuff with significant responsibilities, but he still likes a laugh and more often than not his conversation is peppered with (frequently ribald) humour. He calls a spade a spade, and does not belong to the sugar-coating school of false bonhomie. He's like Brian Hart: what you see is what you get. His background of finding funding for the team encompasses some of the sheer good fortune that many only dream of, but is nonetheless impressive.

'It's all about identifying and implementing places where Jordan can earn money,' he stresses. 'Obviously it's principally sponsorship. And I suppose

Despite the care with which the best F1 plans are laid, things don't always go to plan. Irvine ended the 1994 Italian GP at Monza in the gravel trap . . . (ICN UK Bureau)

that servicing the sponsorships comes under me . . .' He pauses and his face creases into its habitual smile. 'But I'm not a very good executive hand-holder because I tend to speak my mind rather too often! People don't mind when they get used to it. So other people do the servicing side of things, but it all comes under me, and Giselle Davis, our press officer, is in charge of all that and answers to me, if you like.

'Then there's the livery of the cars, the motorhome, that sort of general presentation and marketing. The bits and pieces that don't make the car go faster – but which pay for it.'

In 1991 the nascent Jordan team's sponsorship deal with Seven Up was the talk of the paddock. It went down in history as one of those singular liaisons that stays in the memory, like the black and gold John Player Lotuses of the 1970s. Somehow, the combination of a team with so many Irish connotations and the sponsor's Emerald Green colour, allied to Gary Anderson's beautiful 191 and graphic artist Ian Hutchinson's understated but

highly effective livery design, came together to make a significant impact. But beneath the surface all was very far from what it seemed. And the way in which Eddie Jordan handled the whole thing was another significant indication of his innate courage and willingness to gamble in order to move forward.

Phillips is the first to admit that this particular deal didn't pay for much. Though it looked lucrative to outsiders, because of the professionalism with which Jordan approached its racing, the truth was that the Seven Up deal barely amounted to a row of beans. The company invested only $1.1 million in the desperate enterprise, thereby buying itself the sponsorship deal – or steal? – of the century. But Jordan felt that taking only a small amount, and having a title sponsor to boast about, was better than running a car without a title sponsor, and making the financial situation obvious. Besides, he harboured the hope that he could persuade the company to ante up a significant amount more cash in 1992, after the success of its promotional effort in 1991. This was not to be.

It was widely believed that, having got a cheap year's exposure at the highest level, Seven Up decided to pull out rather than yield to Jordan's blandishments to stay for a second season. Apparently not.

'What happened,' Ian Phillips explains, 'was that Pepsi was committed to doing the Michael Jackson Tour in 1992. The regions said that they wanted to continue in F1, and head office said "Okay that's not a problem to us, but this is what you are all paying towards Michael Jackson. If you want to do F1, you've got to find additional budget for that." And they offered us the same deal as we'd had in 1991!

. . . While Fisichella's Brazilian GP three years later also got off to a less than auspicious start. (ICN UK Bureau)

'Although we'd got nothing else, Eddie and I sat down in the greasy spoon café at Silverstone, one very damp Friday in January, and decided that we had to turn it down. They wanted the same deal for the same money, and it was just giving too much away.'

Consider the situation: through 1991 Team Seven Up Jordan had become an established entity, and all of Jordan's publicity and marketing material reflected the collaboration. Not only that, it gave the team a sense of identity, and fixed that in the minds of racegoers the world over. Now Jordan and Phillips were preparing to forego all that, not so much in the hope that

something better might turn up, but because they simply couldn't afford to let themselves be seen to do such a cut-price deal two years in a row.

Sasol signed for eight times the sum we'd turned down a week before

It might have been only $1.1 million – very, very small beer by F1 standards for a title sponsorship – but at the same time it was all they had in terms of serious income at a stage when the debts were massive. It was indeed a courageous and momentous decision to turn Seven Up down. As it turned out, however, it was unquestionably the right one. The luck of the Irish would save Eeejay yet again, and he wouldn't have to wait long for it to happen.

'Eddie made the call on the Friday, saying thank you but no thank you,' Phillips remembers. 'And it's funny. I'd just said to him, "I think things are on the move, the markets are livening up a bit. Particularly in Japan." I was well wide of the mark as far as Japan was concerned. But on the following Tuesday I got an anonymous phone call asking about oil companies. By Friday we had signed Sasol.'

Sasol, the South African national oil company, had decided to enter F1 to generate a means of opening up its trading potential in world markets. It was to prove an ideal partner for Jordan. Phillips still chuckles at the rightness of the situation. There they

were, having turned down Seven Up only after much deliberation, and here was Sasol, all signed and sealed within a week. It was almost too good to be true. 'And, for eight times as much money as we'd turned down the previous Friday! At the time we were turning down $1.1 million and we were £4.5 million in debt and had no idea where the next payment was coming from. We'd never heard of Sasol, but within seven days the deal was done. That was pure luck.'

That relationship with Sasol was always strong, even if it didn't get off to a brilliant start when the team failed to qualify one car, Stefano Modena's, in the South African GP at Kyalami which opened the 1992 season on Sasol's home turf. 'We then went to Brazil, which was a horrendous disaster, where we did three engine changes on Gugelmin's car without it even leaving the pits! The car hadn't even put its wheels on the deck. We did three awful races, though in Mexico Gugelmin qualified eighth on the grid. But then the crankshaft broke on the way to line up for the start!

'We got back from Mexico on the Monday. On the Tuesday Eddie and I went to the Sasol office in London and they signed another two-year deal, with an extension on top of that for a further two years.' Sadly, however, the deal was not destined to last that long,

The colour, spectacle and drama of GP racing is nicely captured at Monaco in 1995, where the two Jordans escaped undamaged as David Coulthard tangled with the Ferraris of Gerhard Berger and Jean Alesi. (ICN UK Bureau)

1996 marked the start of a major new era for the Jordan team. On home ground in Brazil, Rubens Barrichello takes the fight to leader Damon Hill as the Silverstone team's cars race for only the second time in the colours of Benson & Hedges. (ICN UK Bureau)

and why it foundered is another indication of the pace of change within F1. Literally, nothing stands still, and nothing is for ever.

'Of course,' Phillips explains, 'what happened with Sasol's time with us was the change of government in South Africa, where basically all the profitable companies were expected to participate in the restructuring of South Africa. And politically it was no longer seen as correct for Sasol to keep sponsoring a white, elitist sport.

'But they were a great sponsor. They'd have loved to continue and they remain very good friends to us to this day. They were the only people in the world to make oil from coal, and their technical people were just fascinated by F1. They really bought into it. They bought a dynamometer and installed it over in South Africa, they bought a V8 engine from Brian Hart, and they really got into the whole research and development programme and actually came up with some really good stuff.

'So it was very good, and they worked it very hard everywhere they went. And I think very successfully, too. They rarely came away from a

Early in 1996 the Jordans were a mustard yellow to ensure that monochrome photography and television screens picked out the B&H logos. (ICN UK Bureau)

Grand Prix without a contract in their pocket to supply candle wax to somebody, or whatever. It was terrific, and they were a great, great company to work with. Nice people.'

The Sasol deal finished at the end of 1994, but with Peugeot coming aboard it could not have continued in any case because of conflicts with Peugeot's allegiance to the French Total oil company. 'That was another thing about the Sasol deal. As it happened, it kind of fell right. Sasol wouldn't have left us in the lurch, but because of the restructuring thing in South Africa we had to go with Total anyway. As it happened, Sasol and Total are major business partners in South Africa.'

All this, however, left Jordan Grand Prix without a title sponsor, and that vacancy was not filled until Benson & Hedges came along in 1996.

The team enjoyed its most competitive season in 1997, the year when B&H's gold colours were replaced by a distinctive bright yellow, and the Jordan 197 developed significant downforce and grew snake fangs on the sides of its nose. The fangs were typical Jordan trademarks. They looked to some like the flames that 1950s hot-rodders painted on their cars; but to Jordan they were aggressive and distinctive and the message they gave was, 'We don't care what others think. This is us, take it or leave it.'

Yet again there was fifth place over-

Where the money goes

Budgets vary enormously in F1, which is partly why some teams are more successful than others. In 1997 it cost Jordan a minimum of £18 million to contest the 17-race season.

Building and running the cars, and replacing expendable items such as gearboxes, brakes, and wheels through the course of the season, accounted for £8 million of that. Tyres added another million.

Travel to and from the races – as far flung as Australia, Brazil, Argentina, Canada and Japan, as well as Europe – cost another £3 million, and freight £1 million. And this for a team that enjoys FOCA travel concessions because of finishing within the top 10 in the previous year's Constructors' Championship.

Jordan entertains its clients lavishly at races, via the FIA's Paddock Club facilities. It spends £2 million there every year, but mostly re-charges that out to sponsors.

Back at the Silverstone factory, the annual wage bill was £3 million, and overheads £1 million, while technical development was another half million. The last figure seems surprisingly reasonable, but one should bear in mind that fixed costs such as wages and machinery come from other budgets.

On top of that there are sundries which, Trevor Foster points out drily, 'can mount up quite surprisingly'. The budget for painting the race cars is around £150,000, for example, although that includes continual work to keep up the professional appearance. Refurbishment of the transporters and other support vehicles adds another £65,000. Then there are factors such as capital expenditure. The sort of machinery required to build F1 cars does not come cheap.

The flanks of the Jordan 195 tell the tale of the cost of F1, with precious little space failing to reflect the support of sponsors. (LAT)

all in the Constructors' Championship. But the mere statistics hid some great performances. With a disgruntled Barrichello switching to the new team owned by Jackie and Paul Stewart for 1997, and Martin Brundle being dropped in controversial circumstances, Eddie Jordan opted for youth and inexperience as he partnered the talented Italian newcomer Giancarlo Fisichella with Michael Schumacher's younger brother Ralf.

We concentrate on making the sponsorship work seven days a week

This 1997 driver line-up was potentially explosive. One of the bangs came as early as the Argentinian GP in Buenos Aires in April. It was the third round of the championship, and Jordan's hundredth GP. Schumacher nearly won. Only inexperience – on both his and the team's behalf – and a brush which saw the German take his team-mate out of the race, prevented the great breakthrough marking the team's century. Nevertheless, Ralf finished an honourable third, within 12 seconds of the winner, World Champion-to-be Jacques Villeneuve.

In the second half of the season, Fisichella led the German GP for a while and, having been overtaken by the flying Gerhard Berger, was beginning to mount a fresh challenge to the Austrian's Benetton when his left rear tyre exploded. Though Fisichella was robbed of deserved points on that occasion, he later finished second to Michael Schumacher in Belgium's rain. Throw in third in Canada, fourths at Imola, Monza and Austria, plus Schumacher Jnr's fifths in Britain, Germany, Hungary and Austria, and the picture of an improving team emerged strongly. With just a little better luck or experience, said paddock pundits, Jordan could have joined the winning elite.

The dramatic increase in funding for the 1997 season brought changes not just in the team's on-track performance but in several other management areas, though Phillips believes that Jordan Grand Prix was operating at 'a fairly high level anyway, from the commercial side of things. Yes, we could do with a couple more people. But I think the way we operate is that we integrate people into what we are doing a little bit, rather than holding them at arms' length. We are not too strong on executive hand-holding. We like people to muck in.'

That might seem a slightly cavalier attitude and not to every corporate heavy-hitter's taste. But there is no doubt that at races nobody is better than Jordan Grand Prix when it comes to entertaining guests or sponsors. The team and its commercially imaginative boss have continuously been surrounded by personalities from other areas. Rock star Chris Rea is a motor racing fan of the deepest level, somebody who truly

Brundle again, this time at Monza later that year, when he underlined his character by giving the fans what they wanted. (Formula 1 Pictures)

106

Man and motor. At the end of 1996 Eddie Jordan could justly take pride in his best-ever season of F1 racing, while looking forward to an even better year to come. (Formula 1 Pictures)

understands the sport and its heritage, and has long been a close friend of both Jordan and his team. In 1997 he was joined by others such as Chris de Burgh. Page Three girl Melinda Messenger was also called upon to liven up the show on occasion: Jordan has bankable ideas on attracting media attention.

It's good at etiquette too. If you enter the team's motorhome area in the paddock, each dining table is neatly marked for the use of specific sponsors and their guests, such as venture capitalist Team GdZ, or Hewlett Packard. This is a sensible courtesy beyond price, and particularly appreciated when you see sponsors of other more opulent teams, who are paying more for less, wandering around looking for somewhere to sit at feeding time. Nothing is more detrimental to delicate images and egos.

'What we try to do is make sure that people get to touch F1,' says Phillips. 'We do have a massive input of people over the three days of a Grand Prix, even if it's just to come and have a drink at the motorhome and a quick walk round the garage. It's such a rare experience for people, and we have to shuffle around the 22 guest passes or whatever it is for a Grand Prix.'

This is sound economics too, to look after even the smallest sponsor or supplier, on the basis that the little guy who chips in his contribution and enjoys his look round on a Friday, may

well want to increase his commitment in ensuing years so that he can have a longer looksee on a Saturday or Sunday. At Jordan this corporate massaging is done with engaging style.

'What's different now,' Phillips continues, 'is that having got major corporate backers, like Benson & Hedges and Mastercard, necessarily there is not as much room for little people as there was before. We mustn't lose sight – we don't want to lose sight – of the fact that those are the people who kept us going. We mustn't lose sight of trade people and little sponsors, because you never know. Rainy days, and all the rest of it. And they did support us so wholeheartedly during the

really, really dark times that it would be wrong for us to kick them out and say that we've got more than we need now. We'll never have more than we need.

'We've got to try and keep the whole thing bubbling. It hasn't been easy, and what we now do is use test days an awful lot more. We can probably have up to 300 people at tests at Silverstone, for example, if we wanted. That gives them close involvement and a lot of them find that it's easier and more enjoyable than the actual Grand Prix itself because there is much less hassle and the drivers are more relaxed.

'What we try never to lose sight of is what we had to do in 1991. We want to make the thing work seven days a week so that what happens at the track at weekends is a bonus. In 1991 we were one of 18 teams that were going there, four of which had to pre-qualify on a Friday morning. And if you didn't get past that hour on a Friday morning Mr Seven Up, sitting outside the gate, simply couldn't come in. You didn't get your passes until you got past pre-qualifying, and there were no guarantees to anybody. So what we had to do was concentrate our energies on making sure that the sponsorship was working all the time. It wasn't just about what was happening at the race track. We did it all quite well. And I think that by and large we've managed to keep that going.'

Chapter 5

Making it all come together

When Giancarlo Fisichella and Ralf Schumacher took to the track in 1997, and exploited the improved competitiveness of Gary Anderson's attractive 197, it was yet another step in Jordan's evolution. Jordan had started as a small race team that constructed its own cars and primarily had itself to satisfy. But now it was growing into something much bigger and potentially less controllable. There were shrewd men at the helm however. While Eddie Jordan and Ian Phillips looked after the funding, and Gary Anderson remained the architect of its increasing technological strength, race team director Trevor Foster was also a vital part of the glue that held the developing company together and planned for its brightening future.

Foster is another of those characters both steeped in motorsport and familiar with its darker side. Back in 1973, like Phillips, he was touched deeply by the tragedy that befell Roger Williamson, for whom he had worked as a mechanic. Four years later he experienced the same thing all over again when that other underrated star, Welshman Tom Pryce, was killed racing for Shadow in the South African GP at Kyalami. Then in 1980 his F2 protege Markkus Hoettinger was killed in a freak accident at Hockenheim, when he was struck by a wheel from Derek Warwick's Toleman.

Foster is not the sort to push his own cause at people. He's a listener and a thinker. Words such as loyalty and integrity embarrass him, but they are apposite. His career encompasses the time with Williamson and Tom Wheatcroft, then spells with the Shadow and Tyrrell F1 teams in the 1970s. In 1982 he was persuaded back after the Hoettinger incident by Brian de Zille, to run Pegasus Motorsport's F3 programme around Brian's son Graham. By one of racing's happier coincidences their Team GdZ Capital company is an enthusiastic sponsor of

Jordan's F1 enterprise. After moving on to Tim Stakes's Swallow Racing F3 team for 1986, Foster finally yielded to Eddie Jordan's offers of employment for 1988.

'Face-to-face it would be 1986, I guess, when I first met Eeejay properly,' he recalls. 'That was the first time he walked straight up to me rather than nodding across the F3 paddock. We'd never really had an actual conversation up until then. That was the first time I met him, and he came and offered me a job to run his F3 team. At that time I decided against it because, to be fair, he had this reputation of being very much a hustler and this, that and the other, and I wasn't sure if I wanted to make the switch.'

But they kept in touch, and at the end of 1987 Jordan told him that he was planning to resurrect his F3000 operation, based around Johnny Herbert. Jordan would have run Johnny anyway, after their F3 success together that season, but approaching Foster was a typically shrewd move. Dave Benbow was leaving to work for Tom Walkinshaw's TWR outfit, and the F3000 programme had collapsed around Tomas Kaiser partway through 1987 and all the equipment had been sold off. Jordan knew that Foster was a big fan after giving Johnny his first taste of F3 when he'd tested him for Pegasus Motorsport as part of his prize for winning the Formula Ford Festival in 1985.

'At the time Eddie said I could either do the F3000 or the F3, so I agreed to go on the basis that I could work with Johnny because I did rate him highly. I went to work for EJR in January 1988.'

First time around the relationship lasted five happy and successful years, but by early 1993 Foster had very much had enough and was looking for a way out. A deal was brokered for him to switch to Lotus, where Herbert was still racing. The reasons for Foster's dissatisfaction and resultant restlessness highlighted Eddie Jordan's most frustrating side: an unwillingness at times to listen and to invest.

If he doesn't like the subject he simply won't concentrate

As Phillips once pointed out, 'Eddie is extremely fair, but there can be occasions when he is extremely frustrating. His biggest weakness in life is an inability to concentrate if he's not interested in the subject. However important it is, if he's not interested in it, getting his attention is very, very difficult. And sometimes I have to use shock tactics to get there. But we do.'

So, in a roundabout way that separated them for the best part of a year, did Foster. 'Basically what happened was that my role in F3000 had been team manager and to run the team logistically, but also to be a race engineer and responsible for engineering. That was my role and Paul Crosby was employed part-time to engineer the second car. And then the organisation had grown and it had gone into a situation where I was filling two roles really.

'The first time, in 1991, when there

were still only 45 people and we did little testing, you could still do the two roles. But as the team had then started to grow and we wanted to improve the show with Yamaha aboard for 1992, I spoke to Eddie about it and told him that I couldn't do the two jobs any more. I was not devoting enough time, in my opinion, to make the management side of it good. And I mean by that, looking after the team and making sure everything was right on that side.

'I also needed to be able to pick up the set-up sheet on a Thursday morning and turn my head into a race engineer, before Sunday night closing the book and then not picking it up again until the Thursday of the next race or for the next test session. I felt that the role had suddenly grown so much bigger, and we were employing more and more people, that I couldn't do both jobs any more.

'So I went to see Eddie and explained that realistically I needed to move onward and upward, so we either had to make my role purely a management role, which would mean employing another race engineer. Or me concentrating more on race engineering and bringing in a team manager.' The latter scenario would effectively have meant demoting himself but it didn't matter; Jordan wasn't listening.

'For whatever reason, Eddie didn't see it that way. We talked about it for some time but he was intransigent about it and wanted me to stick with running the cars but didn't want to

The lobby at Jordan GP combines high-tech appearance with quiet welcome. (LAT)

112

employ a team manager as well as myself. So in the end I was disillusioned from my own point of view because I felt that I could no longer fulfil either role to my own personal satisfaction.

'At that point Peter Collins had been talking to me about taking a senior role at Team Castrol Lotus and taking some of the disciplines we had at Jordan, such as cost control, running a small ship and running it properly, making the books balance etc, as part of his rebuilding package to take the team forward again.

'I did spend quite a lot of time talking to Eddie about my problem, and after I'd signed an agreement with Peter, about two or three days before I was due to leave, Eddie brought me in and said: "Listen, I'll do what you want to do." But I said I had already made my decision and signed the agreement, and my family was all in moving to Norfolk mode. It was too late to turn back now.

'Ironically, as I felt, Eddie ended up employing John Walton as team manager and employing Tim Wright as a race engineer, so he did end up doing what he was fighting against all the time.'

But, crucially, Jordan had the sense to ask Foster what he thought should be done before he left. Foster suggested that chief mechanic 'John-Boy' Walton should take over as team manager because he was the perfect man for the job and deserved the

Floor space, as with all F1 teams, is kept immaculate even while the race cars are being rebuilt. (LAT)

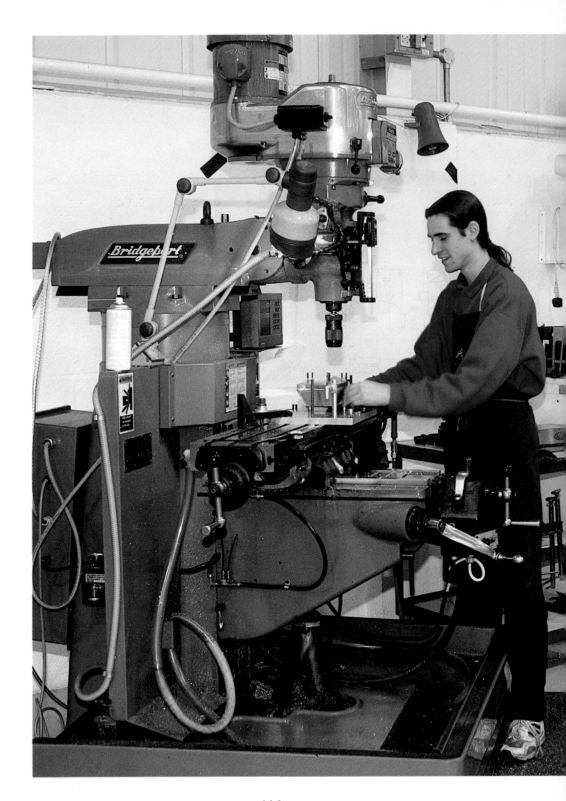

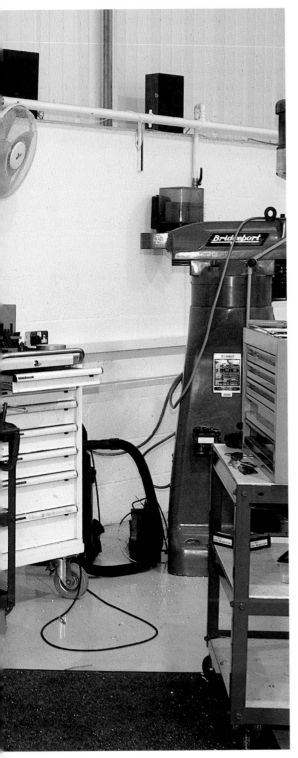

All aspects of F1 car manufacture call for high levels of skill and commitment from team members. (LAT)

opportunity to give it a shot. So even when he had created a situation in which he was about to lose a good man, Jordan was smart enough to let him go without rancour, and to ask his advice, even if he acted on it too late to save a situation that need never have arisen. Foster was not the first person to discover that it takes a crisis before Eddie gives some things his total concentration, and Eddie himself maybe realised that by the time he has focused fully, it can be too late.

We're too big for corridor meetings and it's hard not to become distant

In the long run it was a good move for both. For a variety of reasons, many of them linked to Team Lotus's ongoing and ultimately incurable financial problems, Foster's relationship with that team had faltered by the September. He and Jordan had always kept in touch – 'we didn't ring each other every week, but there were three or four times during the year when we'd communicate' – and before long Eddie was wisely asking him to return.

Foster says: 'I think there's an argument to say that when you come back to an organisation, particularly when it's by mutual agreement, you are in a stronger situation than when you left. It's as if you've proved your independence. So what happened when I came back was that Eddie felt there was a need for a senior person on the manage-

ment side to take over the running of the race team and the factory.

'Obviously Eddie is out a lot because, as he has always maintained, he sees himself not only as the shareholder and the owner of the company, but as the leading salesman. And he doesn't need to be here at Jordan Grand Prix to sell; he's the travelling salesman. And if he has to go to Spain to see someone or to Ireland or wherever, he will go. It means drawing in the money to keep the team on a sound and stable financial footing. And that often means that you're not in the office from half eight to half five, five days a week. And therefore the basis was that he wanted someone there to run the race team for him, and liaise with the factory people, while he is away. He needed someone he could trust to feed him the relevant information that you otherwise do lose contact with when you're not there every day.

'One of the biggest things you have to keep reminding yourself – and this concerns Eddie as well – is to get out of the office and go downstairs and let the staff see you. It's almost like watching the congregation see the Pope, you know what I mean? He comes out on the balcony every so often and says, "Hello, my people."

'It's not because Eddie's not busy. He walks through reception in the morning and speaks to the people in reception but other than that he goes home at seven o'clock at night and basically never gets out of his office. And, of

New for 1997 was Michael Schumacher's younger brother Ralf, paired with Giancarlo Fisichella. (ICN UK Bureau)

course, now that we employ 135 people, some of the guys in the workshop might walk around all day saying, "Has Eddie been in this week, I haven't seen him?" and yet he's probably been in every day.

'So consciously you've got to get out there almost every day, or at least once or twice a week, and literally wander round and say, "How are you doing? Is everything okay?"'

The management group comprises Foster as race team director, Anderson as technical director, Phillips as commercial director and Richard O'Driscoll as financial controller.

This intra-company communication is one of the hardest parts as any organisation grows, particularly one that is operating in such a highly competitive environment as Formula 1. 'Obviously you can't have corridor meetings any more as we used to when there were 45 people and you almost were on top of each other,' Foster says, with what sounds like regret in his voice. 'Now it's very difficult not to get too distant.' It's a case of having to become structured in a way that was anathema when the company was small and worked almost by telepathy and without firm scheduling.

'We couldn't survive without the number of people we have today. It's all very well to say, "Let's go back to the days when we had 45 or 50 people, it'll be all right." But those days are gone. And you can't look back. It's like the

Success was not long coming. Ralf Schumacher faces the media after finishing a dramatic third in Argentina. (ICN UK Bureau)

holiday romance, isn't it? It's like when you say, "We had a fantastic holiday 10 years ago. Let's go back and relive it all because it was so good. We'll get the same people together . . ." And you go back and it's almost the holiday from hell! You've changed, they've changed. It's something you can't recreate.

'I look back at those days, and in 1991 and 1992 we were racing with Minardi and Tyrrell. What I'm saying is that they were around our level. We snapped at the tail of Williams and Ferrari and McLaren a couple of times, but we weren't consistently in their league. Now we've bridged that gap a bit more, and in doing so, because we've grown in different ways and kept up more, we've left the Minardis and Tyrrells behind. We probably haven't caught the Williamses yet, but we have tried to get there and they haven't been able to.'

So while growth is necessary and has allowed Jordan Grand Prix to move closer to the Big Four, such development has not been without a price. 'You miss getting involved in everything,' Foster observes. 'You know, you come up through the ranks, and one of the hardest things I've found is that you have to look, but not dive in. I mean, there's a big temptation just to dive in when you see a mechanic changing a gearbox, to help him. But you've got to stand back. In F3000 you could get stuck in during a bit of a drama, but now you can't. All the people know their jobs. You've got to

Behind every great driver . . . Fisichella ponders set-up with his race engineer, Andy Tilley. (Formula 1 Pictures)

let them do things their way.

'My feeling has always been that I don't want people to do exactly everything I do, my way. You set the levels and then you allow them, within reason, to get to it the direction they want to come through. As long as it's achieved in what you feel is a respectable timescale and you get to that level, then basically people get on and do their job. I don't want five clones underneath me all doing exactly what I do, because I'm the first one to admit that I don't do everything, or haven't done everything, perfectly. And by allowing people a bit of individual freedom, we all learn from it.'

In F1 it's fashionable to knock Eddie Jordan, though this is often done in an affectionate manner. But talk to those who work closely with him and it's not hard to see why they stay.

'At times, working with him is inspirational,' Phillips admits, before pausing. 'And those times are just really, really great. Inspirational in every sense of the word, from a business point of view. He's very good about letting you get on with it. And on a day-to-day basis, I probably have to deal with him more than anybody else. He and I are totally non-technical, but probably because I had to go through a period of building race cars with Leyton House, I can guide him a little bit from that point of view. But the technology has gone way beyond me now.'

'He's much more relaxed, in certain ways,' Foster says. 'The leopard never

Big brother is watching over you. Michael and Ralf play to the home crowd in Germany. (ICN UK Bureau)

The factory: Eddie's biggest gamble

'We've grown massively,' Foster says as he looks round Jordan Grand Prix's factory close to Silverstone Circuit. 'When this factory was built in 1991 it was designed to cope with 55 people, something like that. Now we've got 135 working here, so it's had to be altered over the years.'

The factory was another of Eddie Jordan's master strokes. On the face of it, the last capital resource that the team needed when just starting out in F1 was its own factory, especially as it had to fund a year's racing; the old premises within Silverstone Circuit could have got the team by for another year or so. But Jordan had long-range vision, and knew that bricks and mortar would be precisely the sort of sound investment better made sooner rather than later, especially as this was the height of the recession when building projects were few enough that you could get a good price for having the work done. Right then there weren't a lot of people who wanted a 40,000sq ft factory built. As it turned out, had he not made the investment in 1991 things could have been a little easier financially in the short-term, but the factory might never have been built as the monetary problems increased through 1992.

'The factory is a testimony to Eddie,' Phillips says without hesitation. 'My advice in 1991 was to stop building it; it wasn't going to make the car go any faster. But, he said, "We're selling an image here," and he was right. The Silverstone unit would have

sufficed for another two years, really, but he's a gambler, for sure. Hopefully he's not going to have to gamble like that again, not with his own resources anyway. And I don't think we as a management should ever let him do that. If we manage the place so badly that it comes down to that, then it's time to stop! But he is still prepared to take gambles, I think far more so than most people I know in the business. And that's why he will get there.'

'The opportunity arose,' Foster continues. 'The site was exactly where we wanted it to be. We wanted to be near Silverstone, and you couldn't get closer than opposite the main gate. I believe that initially the Spice sportscar team had done the work to get the old Nissen huts knocked down and permission to build, and then either they decided that financially they couldn't take it any further or

126

else decided to take a commercial unit in Brackley, I'm not sure. But suddenly this thing became available. I mean, we barely had enough money to go racing, it was the last thing we needed. But the opportunity was there and, again, Eejay had the balls to go for it.

'But I don't think even Eddie, if you asked him now, would risk as much as he did then. It's one of those things where you're on the slope and you can't get off it. The thing's going faster and faster. It's like a bobsleigh, and you think at some point, "Jeez, I'm almost out of control here, but I daren't get off because I might break my arm, and if I stay on it there's a chance I might just get to the bottom." And that's the reality of it. I think that's where Eejay was coming from. We were almost out of control in that way; the thing was bigger than we were, bigger than Eddie was. And he was hanging on almost for grim death, and using all of his instinct and guile to hang on and get to the bottom.

'As it was, he got to the bottom, and he was a bit bruised and battered, but apart from that he was able to regroup. There's no doubt that we could have ended up in a Lotus situation where the debts would have been so great that it couldn't ever dig itself out. But we were fortunate that didn't happen.'

One of the best decisions Eddie Jordan ever took was to push ahead with his own bespoke factory in 1990. Situated just opposite the main gate at Silverstone, where EJR once resided, Jordan Grand Prix's headquarters was well established by the start of the 1997 season. (LAT)

changes its spots, and Eddie always wants the deal of the century. And it doesn't matter what deal you do he can always do a better one. And he's probably right in that respect, he always can do a better deal. It doesn't matter how much of a deal we all think we can wheedle out of somebody, whether it be in trucks or generators or motorbikes or mopeds or equipment – whatever deal you think you've beaten a guy or a company down to, Eddie will always be able to get the guy one better. Bigger discount, bigger machine for the same money. Whatever. He can always go one further. That's what he is good at.

At tobacco-banned Hockenheim Fisichella – helped no doubt by the go-faster fangs and the words to go with them – was in contention for victory in the German GP, until fate intervened. (LAT)

'Obviously he's put a dramatic amount of investment in over the last year, and the problem is that Formula 1 is the typical black hole that will just keep going, as with any research industry when you're breaking new levels. And there is still this background of, "Yes, hang on guys. We want to do all this and we want to win. However, the company has to generate income and it must make a profit." Because any company which doesn't have a huge benefactor to fall back on at any moment, must make a profit for its own good, to survive and grow.

'But generally, as he is not so personally involved as he was, Eddie is a lot more relaxed about things. Because of his background, he still sometimes has difficulty in understanding why things cost so much and why we have to invest so much. But that's just something that's ingrown in people.

'Ron Dennis's attitude is totally the

opposite at McLaren, for example. It's always been, "If that's what it needs to win let's do it. I'll find the money somehow." I remember Paul Crosby telling me a story when Ron was working in F3 and running the Marlboro-backed team in 1980. They'd got Marches and it turned out halfway through the season that the chassis to have was the Ralt. Ron's attitude was, "Right, we need Ralts to win. I'm off down there, let's get one." It wasn't in the budget because nobody puts a change of chassis in the budget, but he saw that it was what he needed to do.'

Project Four, Dennis's company, won the British F3 title that year, courtesy of the Swedish driver Stefan Johansson, so the switch paid off. But Foster went on to make a fair point about Eddie Jordan's business acumen.

'You could say that Ron had one or two failures before he sorted out McLaren, and to be fair to Eddie, companywise he hasn't had a failure. He's had a few false starts, but he's never had to fold a company and lay people off or leave people unpaid. At the end of the day he's had to duck and dive but he's done it, and few others can say that. Look back at the heyday of F3, when rivals such as Murray Taylor tried the Ron Dennis approach, and they got blown out of the water. Through his own way, which may not be the conventional way, Eddie's done it and he's here to tell the tale.

'And what you see is what he owns.'

As the Italian was counter-attacking Gerhard Berger for the lead, his left rear tyre sustained a crippling puncture at high speed. (Formula 1 Pictures)

Jordan has always had very strong philosophies about not leasing things. His view is that if you can't buy it outright, then you can't afford it. He is extremely reluctant even to lease trucks or buildings.

Using outside firms we can make cars for a third less than rival teams

Foster makes another interesting observation. 'The £4.5 million debt from 1991 has massively gone, it's been paid for a number of years now. The company turned in respectable profits for its turnover for the last three years, which is what any company has to do.' But it isn't what many aspiring F1 teams do, and that is another tribute to Jordan's acumen. Most F1 teams that get into debt stay in debt, and only get out of it when they collapse. Look at Lotus, Brabham, Pacific or Simtek.

'If you do one of these little exercises and look at pound-for-pound of money spent per budget turnover compared to championship points, Williams is the most successful by far and yet it's not the biggest budget, by far,' Foster continues. 'You could say that Ron Dennis has probably been as successful, or more successful in certain areas, but he's also had a lot more finance at his disposal. If you say, "How much has it cost Jordan to score x amount of championship points this season, and what has it cost, say, Ferrari? That's a difficult one to pinpoint because you can't find out how much Ferrari's overall budget is, but McLaren, Williams and Benetton are fairly well known quantities in that respect. If you plot it out, averaging it over the past four or five years, without a doubt Williams is the best, pound per point.

'So Eddie is also much more aware of his employer's liabilities, if you can put it that way. In other words, looking after his staff.'

This is a factory in which the financial necessities have been identified very thoroughly. Jordan manufactures some of its own suspension components (it was one of the first, if not the first, to use carbon-fibre for the front suspension pushrods), and the new Jordan technical centre in Brackley houses the wind tunnel that Eddie Jordan acquired from Comtech in 1996 and which has been totally modernised. Typically, Jordan did a careful study of Comtech's facilities before moving ahead, and now the centre is fully operational and takes in paying customers on the days when the team does not require it.

Facilities such as wind tunnels and seven or four poster test rigs are seen as vital these days. But Eddie Jordan invests money wisely in such areas. It is not strictly necessary, for example, for an F1 team to manufacturer its carbon-fibre monocoque chassis in-house, and Jordan remains one of the few which has resisted this temptation. It has

After giving Giancarlo a lift back to the pits at Hockenheim, Michael Schumacher made graceful acknowledgement of the quality of the young Italian's performance. (ICN UK Bureau)

done so by choice. 'Our tubs are made by a specialist composite company, Paxford in Huntingdon, that only does F1 work for us,' Foster says.

He agrees that they wanted Jordan to be technology-driven, but it has been a matter of careful consideration what technology it absolutely needs to control for itself, and what it can

A month later Fisichella drove brilliantly to take second place behind Michael Schumacher in the rain-soaked Belgian GP at Spa, matching Jordan's best F1 result. (LAT)

simply plug into from reliable suppliers. 'You could say why haven't we built a 50 per cent wind tunnel, like Williams has, but they cost $8 million. And we don't at this time have $8 million, so we took the next best option that was available to us. It was a lot less than that, but it's given us a step up from where we were, which was the 30 per cent tunnel in Southampton, to this 40 per cent tunnel of our own. We now access any time we like, day or night.

'It's the same with the seven-poster test rig that we have. We can have a car on that and just run it permanently all the time. It's there for the engineers to experiment with, without having to take the car to similar facilities in Bath or Cranfield, which require at least a day's notice so that they can set up the rig. You don't have the situation where you have two days and then you've got to go because another customer is coming in. Our guys have got it full-time.'

Phillips takes up the point. 'When we were talking with Ford about possible engine supply at the end of 1994, Cosworth personnel had come round Jordan Grand Prix and reported that we didn't manufacture anything, we were only a race team. Well, sure, that's what we are, we are a race team. We are a design, research and development enterprise, and a race team. We don't manufacture anything. And hopefully we never will.

'What's the point when there's an industry all over Britain that you can

There is usually a strong story around Jordan. At the 1997 British GP it centred on Sun Page Three girl Melinda Messenger. (Formula 1 Pictures)

hit? I know that Gary would like some more stuff in-house, but at the end of the day it's a bloody good industry in Britain and if you get it built outside you get three things: price, quality and delivery. The three pre-requisites. If you make that sort of thing in-house and mess up any of them, the stuff's in the bin. The material's gone, the man's time has gone, your electricity has gone. Everything. While you can still get it made outside, and we do monitor every area on a quarterly basis to assess cost-efficiency, that's the way we should do it. Who wants to carry a wage bill for 250 people? Eddie would tear his hair out if he actually had to look at that . . .

'Of course, there are several teams that have got that many staff. In the 1980s you had to have them because the industry was saturated, because you'd got March, Ralt, Lola, all that lot making proprietary racing cars. There was no capacity; motor racing was booming everywhere. Jordan was very lucky that the bust time came in 1990, and these people were crying out for work.

'I would say that, notwithstanding Gary's ability to engineer things fairly simply, we still manufacture a car for 30 per cent less than anyone else. A lot of that is down to Gary, but a lot of it is also because of the relationship we have with suppliers. Fixed contracts for doing wishbones for two years at a set price, that sort of thing. It's sensible. It's good housekeeping.'

This was what enabled Jordan Grand Prix to survive from the dark financial days of 1991 through to the middle of the 1994 season when it was finally able to discharge most of the debt that had accrued. The final portion disappeared in 1996 when a major supplier agreed to write off a sum that dated back to 1991. That was how long it took Eddie Jordan's fledgling team to pay for that inaugural season. It's also a graphic illustration of just how tough it is not just to bounce into F1 at a high enough level to attract attention and achieve reasonable results, but to survive long enough to build on such foundations. This is a tough game in which only the smart can prosper.

Keeping a grip on the purse strings is vital for survival. Richard O'Driscoll came aboard as financial controller at the end of 1992, as the money side of the company was growing beyond Eddie's ability to keep track. Still regulating this with part-time accountants on the ad hoc basis he'd used over the years, he had finally come to acknowledge that it was too much for one person to control. Eddie had known O'Driscoll for years as the bank manager at the Allied Irish Bank in Northampton, and as Jordan Grand Prix's financial controller he now took the burden of day-to-day finances off Eddie's shoulders, and prepared projected cashflows.

In the past Eddie had tended to go through it all and say, 'This is what I owe and this is what I've got in the bank, so I'm okay.' But now there was proper planning and O'Driscoll's knowledge of banking helped them to stretch the money as far as it would go, in a much more controlled manner. Jordan Grand Prix at last had really solid foundations.

Chapter 6

Chasing
the big-time

Damon Hill smiled broadly and looked across at Eddie Jordan as he said, 'I'd just like to thank Eddie for continuing his policy of investing in youth . . .'

It was a Friday morning in Austria, and they had just put everyone out of their misery by confirming that they would join forces for 1998. Hill's comment was a jokey reference to his age. At 37 he is relatively old by F1 standards, and in 1997 Jordan had made much of his 'investment' in the youth of Giancarlo Fisichella and Ralf Schumacher.

The fresh alliance, which had proved impossible to engineer a season earlier, was crucial to Jordan Grand Prix's increasingly desperate aspiration to justify itself by winning a Grand Prix.

'There is absolutely no question that a person who has won in excess of 20 GPs brings to this team something unparalleled,' Jordan declared. 'We've never had that opportunity before.'

Hill would not be the first winner of a GP that the team had employed; the Belgian driver Thierry Boutsen had that honour back in 1993. But Hill was its first World Champion, and he was still the reigning title holder when he put his signature to the contract. 'Ralf and Damon are very strong-willed people,' Jordan continued. 'I think we could not possibly have a better opportunity going into 1998. Coupled with the fact that the relationship that is forming now with Mugen-Honda and our own technical advancements that we have been able to invest in, this without any question is way and by far the best opportunity we could ever hope to have.'

But where had the Benson & Hedges money gone? Like Jordan, technical director Gary Anderson had always insisted: 'If you came into F1 today with the view to challenge for the World Championship within three to five years, you simply couldn't do it without a relationship with a major engine manufacturer, as well as the right access from the very start to very high levels of in-house technology.'

It's always been 'come on Damon, when will you come on board again?'

For Anderson that meant investment in the new wind tunnel, the test rigs, and computational fluid dynamics (cfd), all of which Jordan now boasts. 'The whole thing about the car running on the track is the aerodynamics, the roll and pitch and the air load,' he continues. 'And every bump that you go over is important. If you're going at 300kmh it's a very small bump because the thing has so much grip. It'll put a shock in the car but the grip will still be there. And things such as seven-poster test rigs just put all these loads into the car. A complete aero map, complete roll and pitch map, so that the car is actually doing the things on the rig that it does on the track. It has the same tyres it has on the track, so they're also giving an input. It's very complex.

'In Argentina, for example, on the Friday we were gathering packets of data that would be running at the Silverstone factory while we were sitting back after practice. Then we'd see what the car was doing and work through Friday night and Saturday morning to try to work out three or four different set-ups.'

Jordan thus now has all of the facilities to monitor its car at similar levels to the established Top Four. And the team clearly has hopes that when Honda itself comes back into F1, it will be with them. That would be the final icing on the cake.

'Now that we have all those toys, we have this blend of youth and experience and I have to believe that's best for us,' Jordan says. And he is clearly delighted that a driver of Hill's proven calibre will be leading the team.

'After Damon turned us down in 1996 our talks never really stopped. The fact that he lives in Dublin obviously helps because we meet a little socially. We play a little bit of rock and roll together as well. There's always been a thing, "Come on Damon, when are you going to get on board again?"' Jordan gave Hill his first taste of F3 back in 1985, and ran him in F3000 via the EJR link with Middlebridge in 1991, though observers always felt a degree of tension in the relationship.

'At Magny-Cours I spoke to Damon when I realised what was happening with regard to the Fisichella affair. I wasn't sure whether he was going or whether we'd be in a position to sell him back to Benetton. Then certainly again at Silverstone, at the post-race rock concert. We then spoke to him when he was on holiday in France, and there were several meetings after that. It was basically finalised at Monza and documented that Tuesday.'

What happened to hasten things was that Hill hitched a ride back from

Shake on it, champ. Ralf Schumacher publicly welcomes former World Champion Damon Hill aboard at the Albert Hall launch of the 1998 Jordan Mugen-Honda. (Formula 1 Pictures)

the Italian GP on the plane chartered by Jordan sponsor, Brian de Zille. During the flight Hill, Jordan, Anderson and B&H's Nigel Northridge were able to thrash out the details face-to-face. By the time the plane touched down in Oxford the deal was finally agreed after months of prevarication by Hill which had so irritated the Sauber and Prost teams with whom he had also been in negotiation. 'To say we were hijacked would not necessarily be the correct statement,' Jordan smirked, 'but we hijacked each other, so to speak. Damon and I needed to be together in the same place at the same time.'

He firmly denied suggestions that both sides had been obliged to swallow their pride after Hill had decided not to be backed into a corner with Jordan the previous year and had opted instead for his ill-fated liaison with Arrows. 'Humble pie doesn't come into it. In F1 things change so dramatically and quickly. What does come into it is being at all times alert to take the best opportunity when it arises. The opportunity to talk to Damon recurred and it was as a result perhaps of a couple of conversations between Damon and Hirotoshi Honda that really made sure that Damon knew what he wanted to do.

'We've hired Damon to win races. We've hired him to win championships. No other reason. We are in a position where we have a huge new dawn in

Designing to the new narrow-track regulations, which also embraced a return to grooved tyres, Gary Anderson once again penned one of the most elegant F1 cars of the season. (Formula 1 Pictures)

Young lions clawing themselves

Giancarlo Fisichella had played second fiddle to Ralf Schumacher at the start of the 1997 season, content to learn quietly at his own pace. 'It was impressive how he was prepared to do that, and not to go for the carrot of Ralf's lap times,' said Andy Tilley, his race engineer. 'It was the sign of an adult mind. Most drivers would have started going to pieces in such circumstances.'

As his confidence and stature grew, allied to massive publicity in Italy as the emergent White Hope, Fisichella's movie star looks and jaunty walk marked him out as a champion of the future. But not before the team-mates had their celebrated coming together in Argentina, when Fisichella was ahead but got taken off as Ralf accidentally hit his back wheel.

Fisichella was livid. 'I am very angry, but we have discussed the matter within the team.' Schumacher appeared publicly unmoved. Both were given a rocket by Eddie Jordan, who kept a tight lid on the situation as the media smelled a good story. 'Ralf admits that he made a mistake, and he was very clear about it. Very correct,' he insisted.

There was a saying in the F1 paddock around this time that Ralf was so arrogant that even Michael noticed. Gary Anderson had observed even before Argentina that he believed Ralf to be better at this stage of his career than Michael was when he graduated.

Trevor Foster had a more reserved view, but the gist was the same. 'Ralf is his own character, and I think he drove a very good race. A podium finish in only your third Grand Prix is pretty good going. He's very strong mentally, and he's here to do the job. That's all we can ask. Sure, he's made some mistakes, he's finding the limits, and there have been some spins, but that's what the job is all about. He's 18 months younger than Michael was at the same stage of his career, and Michael had the benefit of that extra maturity and a couple of seasons racing in the professional atmosphere of Mercedes-Benz's sportscar team. Just over a year ago Ralf was still racing in Formula 3.

'I said to Eddie when he signed him that I didn't think Ralf was at Michael's level, and that it would take three or six months, depending on how he applied himself. And I have to say that he's doing that very quickly.'

In private Fisichella simply gnashed his teeth. 'As far as I'm concerned, any friendship is finished. From now on he gets the minimum from me that allows me to do a professional job.'

Had legendary American World Champion Mario Andretti seen the incident and its aftermath he would doubtless have chuckled and used the line he came out with when Gilles Villeneuve and Rene Arnoux wheel-banged their way through the 1979 French GP. 'Aw, it's just a couple of young lions clawing themselves.'

Despite the cockiness, Ralf did not have an easy time in 1997. His road driving was a source of regular criticism within the team. On one memorable occasion he treated his mechanics to rides around the Circuit de Catalunya, Barcelona, in his hire car. One, who did not wish to be identified, said: 'It was an object lesson in how not to do it. He was far too rough and he was all over the place, just over-driving the thing.'

What Ralf didn't know was the many of his mechanics were racing men themselves, with backgrounds in Formula Ford 1600, the traditional training ground. Several had a go in the hire car and set faster laps.

For all that, they admired Ralf's sheer determination and raw speed, although patience was a little strained after three off-course excursions at Spa, one of them before the race had even started; and at the Nurburgring where he and Fisichella collided again in the first corner. On that occasion Ralf landed in brother Michael's cockpit, seriously damaging his World Championship prospects. 'He has the speed,' says Anderson who, since Imola 1994, has not been able to watch a race comfortably, 'but he needs to learn to calm himself down a little.'

About Fisichella they all had no doubts. The feeble and expensive attempt to keep him for 1998 was proof of that. Effectively, Jordan had taken him on a one-year lease from Benetton, where then team boss Flavio Briatore had a management deal with his young compatriot. But Eddie hoped that by contesting Benetton's right to sign Fisichella for 1998 he might just hang on to him for another season. It was typical opportunism.

'At Magny-Cours when I realised what was happening with regard to the Fisichella Affair I wasn't sure whether he was going or whether we'd be in a position to sell him back to Benetton. We had been advised that it wasn't a very strong case.' Not a month earlier he had been telling the world the precise opposite. 'We saw it as a test case, and if we were in a position to have won there would probably have been a commercial interest involved.' Meaning that if necessary Jordan would have sold Fisichella back to Benetton, though many within the team found this hard to believe. Had Jordan won the case it would surely have retained the Italian for a second season. Instead, like Michael Schumacher, he would become 'the one who got away'.

With its dramatic new colour scheme, the 1997 Jordan-Peugeots made a huge impact throughout the season. As did their two young drivers Ralf Schumacher and Giancarlo Fisichella, sometimes on each other. (LAT)

front of us, particularly with Mugen-Honda. Jordan is in a position, with Ralf Schumacher and Damon Hill, where if we cannot win races in 1998 it will be a very, very bitter blow for us.'

Despite the significance of the latest moves, Ian Phillips believes that Jordan Grand Prix is essentially the same company that started on the F1 road seven years earlier. 'I'd like to think that the spirit of the company hasn't changed since the early days, because the spirit is Eejay. Okay, we have to be more respectable if you like, because we are representing major corporations after all. So the attitude has to change a bit, but I don't think we've lost the element, the spirit of adventure if you like, that is Jordan.

'At the end of the day, yes it's a business and it's a business with a lot of money at stake, but there is a sporting element to it and sport is there to be enjoyed. There have to be winners and losers, but just because an hour or a day after a dismal performance we have regained our sense of humour, doesn't mean that the dismal performance hasn't killed us. Because it does. It really, really does. You can't wipe that performance from the record books. It's there, there's nothing you can do about it. What you've got to do is be positive towards the next one, and use it as a motivation to do better.

'And I think that's what we are capable of doing. Eddie recovers more quickly than most, but that's not to say that he doesn't care. It actually affects him a bit more than anybody.

'We mustn't lose the sense of fun. It would be wrong to do that, and I think it's a total fallacy to say that because we are a team with a smile on our faces it doesn't mean that we are taking it seriously. We are. We are deadly serious. But, you know, what is wrong with enjoying what we do? Luckily after eight years working with the company, I still sing in the car on the way to work! Driving home I might want to get very drunk, but . . .'

In the paddock Jordan's continuing bonhomie stands out. But that brings its own problems. 'The burden we carry is that the public sees Jordan as much more successful than we actually are, and we would love to be able to balance that out. But from a media

Like Ian Phillips, Jordan's race director Trevor Foster has seen most aspects of motor racing in his time. All that remains is to be a key part of an F1 victory. (Sutton Motorsport)

For the Englishman, Jordan is a lifeline at a time when he desperately wants to prove again his ability to win races. 'If I don't, I shall be very, very disappointed,' he said before the season began. (LAT)

point of view I think we have been fairly successful. And with the media or sponsors we always say to everybody, "Don't be afraid to ask. Whatever kind of stunt you want us to pull, ask. And if we say no, you're no worse off." And now people I don't think even bother to ask the McLarens and Williamses; they just come straight here.

'That has helped to build Jordan, because whenever there is a tobacco story on television, bang! There's a Jordan going round. Whenever you want to see a racing car on the "Generation Game" or "You Bet!", it's always a Jordan. So I think we've done pretty well from that point of view. But as the person who is responsible overall for building the brand, I think there comes a time when we've got to start justifying that. Which is what we want to do.'

With Damon Hill aboard, the team's first big success is guaranteed to grab the headlines. It's a thought that makes Phillips smile and start laughing happily again. 'The day when it happens is going to be wild, for sure! It's going to be a great day. I'll probably sit in a corner and cry my eyes out for about 24 hours. Even after 10, 11 years of team involvement the emotion of

For the German, 1998 was the chance to beat an established former champion, and thereby to underline his own claim to the throne occupied twice by his older brother. (LAT)

competing – win, lose or draw – is still very high. And very draining too. I think I've lost my passion for motorsport. It's become a business. But seeing Michael Schumacher at his best, at Spa or Monaco – not Jerez! – I remember what I enjoy best about all this. Just watching that man drive is numbing.

'I know from my own point of view that for the last five years the actual passion has faded. Partly it's over exposure, I guess. And maybe you just get too close. What I used to love in my first days as a journalist was that I'd go to Silverstone to test my Clubmans car and find the new BRM being given a shakedown, because they didn't do launches then. There'd be this ghastly green lorry with something being wheeled out of it! There were always surprises, and today perhaps everything's all a bit too predictable and boring. We all do new car launches, which nobody in the media is really interested in! But it's what the sponsors want; there has to be a show. That's where it's all changed. Very few people are interested now in the nuts and bolts of the car. How much call is there for anyone to write anything technical? You need something like the Spice Girls or Jamiroquai . . .'

The Benson & Hedges deal may have been the answer to Jordan's dreams, but it carries with it a requirement for much media hype. And it has posed some tough questions.

'I think the biggest question,' Phillips admits, 'is the one everybody has always asked: how strong was Eddie's commitment to the company and to going forward and investing to make it successful? I think we've answered it pretty well though the statistics would say not. People wanted to know whether we could spend that money wisely.

'Now in that first year, 1996, the money wasn't big at all. But it was enormous from the Jordan point of view. It actually wasn't as big as Sasol had been.' Accurate sources say it was £5 million.

Pre-season testing is crucial. And teams which can get going as soon as possible have the valuable opportunity to steal an advantage by familiarising themselves thoroughly with their car before the first race. (LAT)

'But I think we did spend it wisely. We spent three months identifying internally where we were going wrong, and what we needed to do to strengthen the company on the technical side. Things weren't going well in a lot of directions. We were just generally under-achieving in everything that we did.'

These were hard days for the team, and Gary Anderson's absence from the British GP that year created a huge amount of speculation. It transpired that he had been 'rested' by Jordan, forced to have a break from his penchant for taking so much of the load on his own broad shoulders. At the same time, however, the 1997 budget had already been agreed, which allowed the team to plan the way forward with confidence.

'We had to make sure that the 1997 car was really good,' Phillips continued, 'and more resources were put into it. That was effectively why Gary stopped going racing. First of all we said he had to take a holiday – he hadn't had one in six years because he was all things to all men. He'd asked for more people back in 1993, but it hadn't really happened, and I think everybody gets to the stage where you are tired and need a damn good rest. At

Desperate for Damon

The failure to have won a Grand Prix consumes the Jordan team like a rash that demands constant scratching, and in the 1996 World Champion Damon Hill the management sees a soothing balm.

As usual, commercial director Ian Phillips pulls no punches: 'Beyond his proven abilities as a driver, it's his experience in actually knowing how to win. You've got to understand that though we have all experienced that outside of F1, all of us here, individually and collectively, lack that in F1. There isn't one of us has ever experienced winning a Grand Prix.

'We sometimes wonder if maybe there is something we are doing wrong. It's difficult to put your finger on it but we are very conscious of the fact that we never have. Damon has, and winning brings a certain amount of confidence with it, too. It's perhaps an all-round change of attitude to "I'm used to being a winner and I want to be a winner again," whereas perhaps you might say we have still been at the starry-eyed stage, "Gee, we're actually here in F1!" Obviously it's not quite as naïve as that, but we're looking to him to be the catalyst for an attitude that says we are going to every race to try and win it.'

The 1997 season gave the team genuine hope that victory is close at hand. But, Phillips says candidly: 'Although we had a bloody good year with Schumacher and Fisichella, we all felt round about the middle stage of the season that, had we had Damon in the team, we would have been winning races. Argentina is the first one that I think we could have won, but we could genuinely say that with the right combination, Damon and A.N. Other, we could have won a couple.

'Winning is an attitude, and it's an attitude that we are desperate to acquire, and we hope that Damon is going to be our

lever towards that. He was at Williams for four years, and he knows an awful lot of things.

'The biggest disappointment for us in 1997 was that we were still only fifth in the World Championship although we had a car that for two-thirds of the season was capable of winning. That's what we've got to translate, and Damon is going to be a key element to doing it.'

It's all smiles here, but would Damon and the little brother of his own personal nemesis actually hit it off? That was but one of the fascinating questions at the start of the 1998 season. (LAT)

the same time as a company we'd come to various conclusions on how to invest the money, and that it should go on people and technology. And even though the statistics show that we yet again finished fifth in the championship, we were an all-round better company. We had a far better product and we performed like a top five team rather than inheriting it or being lucky to be there. We definitely matured.

He is a success and is allowed the trappings of that success

'And I think that we can proudly say that the money wasn't spirited away, that it was invested in the company and it was there for everybody to see. That was an achievement. We should be proud of that and it should shut some of the people up who've always been convinced that the money was going in the wrong direction. I think the fact that we've taken Damon on top of that shows that the commitment is there.'

It's easy to be cynical, expecting Eddie Jordan to be motivated solely by financial aspects, and to forget the fire with which he first tackled his F1 project. 'The problem is that when you get a reputation it's very hard to lose it,' Phillips agrees. 'It's what he built up over a period of 10 years before he came into F1. Yes, he was very successful making money out of motor racing. What's the problem in that? The problem is he was very up-front about it.'

Another is that in 1992 he was perceived to have little interest other than to recoup his own personal investment in his team at the earliest possible opportunity. There was a story doing the rounds back then, the truth of which nobody has ever satisfactorily resolved. According to paddock tittle tattle, as his team was struggling with debt Eejay was considering buying a house nearer London and was said to have received details from an estate agent of an extremely opulent house in Hampstead, not far from the Golders Green side of the heath. It's price was variously reported as £2 million or £4 million, depending on your taste for inflation. Eddie has always pooh-poohed the story, but the flight back from that year's Mexican GP took travellers via Paris, and during a coach transfer across the airport he was his usual jocular and derisive self as the banter was on full flow. That is, until the following conversation took place with a journalist.

Jordan: 'You tabloid expletive. Are you still digging the dirt and filth?'

Journalist: 'Tell me Eddie, what shade of green were your cars last year?'

Jordan: 'What the expletive has that got to do with anything?'

Journalist: 'Nothing much. I was just wondering whether it was Golders green, that's all . . .'

Whereupon occurred the only recorded instance in which Edmund Jordan lapsed into complete and absolute public silence . . .

'He's been successful and he's allowed to have the trappings of that success,' agrees Phillips, who insists to this day that he has no inkling of the veracity or otherwise of the story. 'What is the problem with that? But that mustn't be confused with his commitment to the team, which has been total.'

As Jordan Grand Prix's fortunes continued to improve, so its face inevitably continued to change as it matured. 'Technically, F1 is the only place to be, because that is the forefront of it,' Foster says. 'I used to love the engineering of taking a production car and doing the little bits and pieces. Like with the Reynards at EJR, we were the first to blow floors using the exhaust gases to improve the aerodynamics, things like that. And then we did the short sidepods. Lots of other little bits and pieces. And that was quite a nice little thing to do.

'In 3000 you're like a small yacht trying to sail across the Channel, and you can change direction and do things very quickly. In F1 it's almost like you're on an oil tanker and you've got this huge thing and you're trying to steer a course and you've got to think miles ahead. You can't just suddenly turn left.

'You want to keep it fairly streamlined and quick-reacting and all that, but it is harder. And we've all got to educate ourselves. In my section it's no good just me knowing what's going on and what I think; you've got to keep feeding it down all the time. And I'm sure there are people who think we don't feed down enough. You are trying to strike that balance, on the need-to-know basis. Obviously people on the shop floor are informed enough to keep their input and their enthusiasm alive and their interest going, but at the same

Damon Hill said he was delighted to get back behind the wheel after the winter lay-off. At the beginning of February, just after his wife Georgie had given birth to their fourth child, a second daughter, he expressed himself delighted with his first serious run in the car at Barcelona. In particular he praised the handling of the car, and its progressive behaviour on the grooved tyres which many had expected to create inconsistent cornering performance. (LAT)

time you obviously can't tell them everything because there are some things that are confidential or haven't been decided or agreed. So you've got this flow of information. We tend to think that we have too many meetings, but communication is everything.

'If you look at when things go wrong, if you trace it back it's nearly always because of poor communication. Somebody didn't tell; one guy didn't know what the other guy was doing. One thought somebody else was covering it, and neither were doing it. You can't really communicate too much, I don't think.'

When he looks at his company today, Eddie Jordan smiles. 'We have more than 135 people on the payroll, and I always said I would be out the door when it got to 100. Everybody in the office reminds me of that and asks me when am I leaving. Now I tell them it's when we get to 250! Maybe it was naïve, maybe lack of experience, I'm not sure.

'I had in mind that I didn't want to increase, but there are certain things that you have to do on your own and which you can't give out to people to do. Maybe in the carbon area, certainly in the wind tunnel. The research and development with the wind tunnel has taken 25 to 30 people extra and maybe I hadn't envisaged having them before. But we are still over the 100 mark even taking them out, because Jordan Technology is a separate company but interlinked, naturally, through the group. I always consider that the total group, which is actively involved in the racing, is the 45.'

Irreverent he may be, but he is also smart enough to see which side his bread is buttered. He was one of the first of seven teams to sign the controversial 1997 Concorde Agreement, not wishing to spit in the soup and upset the sport's governing body. Crusading is something he pragmatically leaves to others. It's one of the reasons why he will always survive.

Phillips harks back to a favourite point. 'The biggest burden that Jordan Grand Prix carries is that on the back of Eddie's personality we built a brand which is far greater than our results would ever have justified. And people expect us to be winning. But that doesn't happen overnight. I don't know how long it took Frank Williams to win a race, but it was a long time. We started the company in the depths of the biggest recession that most living people can ever remember. There were 16 teams. Of the people who came in since, only Sauber and Jackie Stewart have survived, and Sauber came in fully paid for by Mercedes-Benz and Jackie had Ford behind him. I think that says a lot for Jordan.

'I believe that Eddie is the last genuine privateer to enter Formula 1. I just don't see that it can happen again in our working lifetime. I can't see that it will ever happen at all.'

Appendix 1

Jordan –
race results

The accompanying results table includes all the Formula 1 race results achieved by Jordan-entered Grand Prix cars from 1991 to the final round of the 1997 season.

Key to abbreviations:

Q – did not qualify; R – retired; FL – Fastest lap; P – Pole.

1991

10 Mar   US GP, Phoenix

A. de Cesaris	Jordan-Ford 191	Q
B. Gachot	Jordan-Ford 191	10

24 Mar   BRAZILIAN GP, Interlagos

A. de Cesaris	Jordan-Ford 191	R
B. Gachot	Jordan-Ford 191	13

28 Apr   SAN MARINO GP, Imola

A. de Cesaris	Jordan-Ford 191	R
B. Gachot	Jordan-Ford 191	R

12 May   MONACO GP, Monte Carlo

A. de Cesaris	Jordan-Ford 191	R
B. Gachot	Jordan-Ford 191	8

2 Jun   CANADIAN GP, Montreal

A. de Cesaris	Jordan-Ford 191	4
B. Gachot	Jordan-Ford 191	5

16 Jun   MEXICAN GP, Mexico City

A. de Cesaris	Jordan-Ford 191	4
B. Gachot	Jordan-Ford 191	R

7 Jul   FRENCH GP, Magny-Cours

A. de Cesaris	Jordan-Ford 191	6
B. Gachot	Jordan-Ford 191	R

14 Jul   BRITISH GP, Silverstone

A. de Cesaris	Jordan-Ford 191	R
B. Gachot	Jordan-Ford 191	6

28 Jul   GERMAN GP, Hockenheim

A. de Cesaris	Jordan-Ford 191	5
B. Gachot	Jordan-Ford 191	6

11 Aug   HUNGARIAN GP, Hungaroring

A. de Cesaris	Jordan-Ford 191	7
B. Gachot	Jordan-Ford 191	9/FL

25 Aug   BELGIAN GP, Spa-Francorchamps

A. de Cesaris	Jordan-Ford 191	R
M. Schumacher	Jordan-Ford 191	R

8 Sep   ITALIAN GP, Monza

A. de Cesaris	Jordan-Ford 191	7
R. Moreno	Jordan-Ford 191	R

22 Sep   PORTUGUESE GP, Estoril

A. de Cesaris	Jordan-Ford 191	8
R. Moreno	Jordan-Ford 191	10

29 Sep   SPANISH GP, Barcelona

A. de Cesaris	Jordan-Ford 191	R
A. Zanardi	Jordan-Ford 191	9

20 Oct   JAPANESE GP, Suzuka
A. de Cesaris   Jordan-Ford 191   R
A. Zanardi   Jordan-Ford 191   R
3 Nov   AUSTRALIAN GP, Adelaide
A. de Cesaris   Jordan-Ford 191   8
A. Zanardi   Jordan-Ford 191   9

1992

1 Mar   SOUTH AFRICAN GP, Kyalami
S. Modena   Jordan-Yamaha 192   Q
M. Gugelmin   Jordan-Yamaha 192   11
22 Mar   MEXICAN GP, Mexico City
S. Modena   Jordan-Yamaha 192   R
M. Gugelmin   Jordan-Yamaha 192   R
5 Apr   BRAZILIAN GP, Interlagos
S. Modena   Jordan-Yamaha 192   R
M. Gugelmin   Jordan-Yamaha 192   R
3 May   SPANISH GP, Barcelona
S. Modena   Jordan-Yamaha 192   Q
M. Gugelmin   Jordan-Yamaha 192   R
17 May   SAN MARINO GP, Imola
S. Modena   Jordan-Yamaha 192   R
M. Gugelmin   Jordan-Yamaha 192   7
31 May   MONACO GP, Monte Carlo
S. Modena   Jordan-Yamaha 192   R
M. Gugelmin   Jordan-Yamaha 192   R
14 Jun   CANADIAN GP, Montreal
S. Modena   Jordan-Yamaha 192   R
M. Gugelmin   Jordan-Yamaha 192   R
5 Jul   FRENCH GP, Magny-Cours
S. Modena   Jordan-Yamaha 192   R
M. Gugelmin   Jordan-Yamaha 192   R
12 Jul   BRITISH GP, Silverstone
S. Modena   Jordan-Yamaha 192   R
M. Gugelmin   Jordan-Yamaha 192   R
26 Jul   GERMAN GP, Hockenheim
S. Modena   Jordan-Yamaha 192   Q
M. Gugelmin   Jordan-Yamaha 192   15
16 Aug   HUNGARIAN GP, Hungaroring
S. Modena   Jordan-Yamaha 192   R
M. Gugelmin   Jordan-Yamaha 192   10
30 Aug   BELGIAN GP, Spa-Francorchamps
S. Modena   Jordan-Yamaha 192   15
M. Gugelmin   Jordan-Yamaha 192   14

13 Sep   ITALIAN GP, Monza
S. Modena   Jordan-Yamaha 192   Q
M. Gugelmin   Jordan-Yamaha 192   R
27 Sep   PORTUGUESE GP, Estoril
S. Modena   Jordan-Yamaha 192   13
M. Gugelmin   Jordan-Yamaha 192   R
25 Oct   JAPANESE GP, Suzuka
S. Modena   Jordan-Yamaha 192   7
M. Gugelmin   Jordan-Yamaha 192   R
8 Nov   AUSTRALIAN GP, Adelaide
S. Modena   Jordan-Yamaha 192   6
M. Gugelmin   Jordan-Yamaha 192   R

1993

14 Mar   SOUTH AFRICAN GP, Kyalami
R. Barrichello   Jordan-Hart 193   R
I. Capelli   Jordan-Hart 193   R
28 Mar   BRAZILIAN GP, Interlagos
R. Barrichello   Jordan-Hart 193   R
I. Capelli   Jordan-Hart 193   Q
11 Apr   EUROPEAN GP, Donington Park
R. Barrichello   Jordan-Hart 193   10
T. Boutsen   Jordan-Hart 193   R
25 Apr   SAN MARINO GP, Imola
R. Barrichello   Jordan-Hart 193   R
T. Boutsen   Jordan-Hart 193   R
9 May   SPANISH GP, Barcelona
R. Barrichello   Jordan-Hart 193   12
T. Boutsen   Jordan-Hart 193   11
23 May   MONACO GP, Monte Carlo
R. Barrichello   Jordan-Hart 193   9
T. Boutsen   Jordan-Hart 193   R
13 Jun   CANADIAN GP, Montreal
R. Barrichello   Jordan-Hart 193   R
T. Boutsen   Jordan-Hart 193   12
4 Jul   FRENCH GP, Magny-Cours
R. Barrichello   Jordan-Hart 193   7
T. Boutsen   Jordan-Hart 193   11
11 Jul   BRITISH GP, Silverstone
R. Barrichello   Jordan-Hart 193   10
T. Boutsen   Jordan-Hart 193   R
25 Jul   GERMAN GP, Hockenheim
R. Barrichello   Jordan-Hart 193   R
T. Boutsen   Jordan-Hart 193   13

15 Aug   HUNGARIAN GP, Hungaroring
R. Barrichello   Jordan-Hart 193   R
T. Boutsen   Jordan-Hart 193   9

29 Aug   BELGIAN GP, Spa-Francorchamps
R. Barrichello   Jordan-Hart 193   R
T. Boutsen   Jordan-Hart 193   R

12 Sep   ITALIAN GP, Monza
R. Barrichello   Jordan-Hart 193   R
M. Apicella   Jordan-Hart 193   R

26 Sep   PORTUGUESE GP, Estoril
R. Barrichello   Jordan-Hart 193   13
E. Naspetti   Jordan-Hart 193   R

24 Oct   JAPANESE GP, Suzuka
R. Barrichello   Jordan-Hart 193   5
E. Irvine   Jordan-Hart 193   6

7 Nov   AUSTRALIAN GP, Adelaide
R. Barrichello   Jordan-Hart 193   11
E. Irvine   Jordan-Hart 193   R

1994

27 Mar   BRAZILIAN GP, Interlagos
R. Barrichello   Jordan-Hart 194   4
E. Irvine   Jordan-Hart 194   R

17 Apr   PACIFIC GP, Aida
R. Barrichello   Jordan-Hart 194   3
A. Suzuki   Jordan-Hart 194   R

1 May   SAN MARINO GP, Imola
R. Barrichello   Jordan-Hart 194   N
A. de Cesaris   Jordan-Hart 194   R

15 May   MONACO GP, Monte Carlo
R. Barrichello   Jordan-Hart 194   R
A. de Cesaris   Jordan-Hart 194   4

29 May   SPANISH GP, Barcelona
R. Barrichello   Jordan-Hart 194   R
E. Irvine   Jordan-Hart 194   6

12 Jun   CANADIAN GP, Montreal
R. Barrichello   Jordan-Hart 194   7
E. Irvine   Jordan-Hart 194   R

3 Jul   FRENCH GP, Magny-Cours
R. Barrichello   Jordan-Hart 194   R
E. Irvine   Jordan-Hart 194   R

10 Jul   BRITISH GP, Silverstone
R. Barrichello   Jordan-Hart 194   4
E. Irvine   Jordan-Hart 194   N

31 Jul   GERMAN GP, Hockenheim
R. Barrichello   Jordan-Hart 194   R
E. Irvine   Jordan-Hart 194   R

14 Aug   HUNGARIAN GP, Hungaroring
R. Barrichello   Jordan-Hart 194   R
E. Irvine   Jordan-Hart 194   R

28 Aug   BELGIAN GP, Spa-Francorchamps
R. Barrichello   Jordan-Hart 194   P/R
E. Irvine   Jordan-Hart 194   R

11 Sep   ITALIAN GP, Monza
R. Barrichello   Jordan-Hart 194   4
E. Irvine   Jordan-Hart 194   R

25 Sep   PORTUGUESE GP, Estoril
R. Barrichello   Jordan-Hart 194   4
E. Irvine   Jordan-Hart 194   7

16 Oct   EUROPEAN GP, Jerez
R. Barrichello   Jordan-Hart 194   12
E. Irvine   Jordan-Hart 194   4

6 Nov   JAPANESE GP, Suzuka
R. Barrichello   Jordan-Hart 194   R
E. Irvine   Jordan-Hart 194   5

13 Nov   AUSTRALIAN GP, Adelaide
R. Barrichello   Jordan-Hart 194   4
E. Irvine   Jordan-Hart 194   R

1995

26 Mar   BRAZILIAN GP, Interlagos
R. Barrichello   Jordan-Peugeot 195   R
E. Irvine   Jordan-Peugeot 195   R

9 Apr   ARGENTINIAN GP, Buenos Aires
R. Barrichello   Jordan-Peugeot 195   R
E. Irvine   Jordan-Peugeot 195   R

30 Apr   SAN MARINO GP, Imola
R. Barrichello   Jordan-Peugeot 195   R
E. Irvine   Jordan-Peugeot 195   8

14 May   SPANISH GP, Barcelona
R. Barrichello   Jordan-Peugeot 195   7
E. Irvine   Jordan-Peugeot 195   5

28 May   MONACO GP, Monte Carlo
R. Barrichello   Jordan-Peugeot 195   R
E. Irvine   Jordan-Peugeot 195   R

11 Jun   CANADIAN GP, Montreal
R. Barrichello   Jordan-Peugeot 195   2
E. Irvine   Jordan-Peugeot 195   3

2 Jul   FRENCH GP, Magny-Cours
R. Barrichello   Jordan-Peugeot 195   6
E. Irvine   Jordan-Peugeot 195   9
16 Jul   BRITISH GP, Silverstone
R. Barrichello   Jordan-Peugeot 195   11
E. Irvine   Jordan-Peugeot 195   R
30 Jul   GERMAN GP, Hockenheim
R. Barrichello   Jordan-Peugeot 195   R
E. Irvine   Jordan-Peugeot 195   9
13 Aug   HUNGARIAN GP, Hungaroring
R. Barrichello   Jordan-Peugeot 195   7
E. Irvine   Jordan-Peugeot 195   13
27 Aug   BELGIAN GP, Spa-Francorchamps
R. Barrichello   Jordan-Peugeot 195   6
E. Irvine   Jordan-Peugeot 195   R
10 Sep   ITALIAN GP, Monza
R. Barrichello   Jordan-Peugeot 195   R
E. Irvine   Jordan-Peugeot 195   R
24 Sep   PORTUGUESE GP, Estoril
R. Barrichello   Jordan-Peugeot 195   11
E. Irvine   Jordan-Peugeot 195   10
1 Oct   EUROPEAN GP, Nurburgring
R. Barrichello   Jordan-Peugeot 195   4
E. Irvine   Jordan-Peugeot 195   6
22 Oct   PACIFIC GP, Aida
R. Barrichello   Jordan-Peugeot 195   R
E. Irvine   Jordan-Peugeot 195   11
29 Oct   JAPANESE GP, Suzuka
R. Barrichello   Jordan-Peugeot 195   R
E. Irvine   Jordan-Peugeot 195   4
12 Nov   AUSTRALIAN GP, Adelaide
R. Barrichello   Jordan-Peugeot 195   R
E. Irvine   Jordan-Peugeot 195   R

1996

10 Mar   AUSTRALIAN GP, Melbourne
R. Barrichello   Jordan-Peugeot 196   R
M. Brundle   Jordan-Peugeot 196   R
31 Mar   BRAZILIAN GP, Interlagos
R. Barrichello   Jordan-Peugeot 196   R
M. Brundle   Jordan-Peugeot 196   12
7 Apr   ARGENTINIAN GP, Buenos Aires
R. Barrichello   Jordan-Peugeot 196   4
M. Brundle   Jordan-Peugeot 196   R

28 Apr   EUROPEAN GP, Nurburgring
R. Barrichello   Jordan-Peugeot 196   5
M. Brundle   Jordan-Peugeot 196   6
5 May   SAN MARINO GP, Imola
R. Barrichello   Jordan-Peugeot 196   5
M. Brundle   Jordan-Peugeot 196   R
19 May   MONACO GP, Monte Carlo
R. Barrichello   Jordan-Peugeot 196   R
M. Brundle   Jordan-Peugeot 196   R
2 Jun   SPANISH GP, Barcelona
R. Barrichello   Jordan-Peugeot 196   R
M. Brundle   Jordan-Peugeot 196   R
16 Jun   CANADIAN GP, Montreal
R. Barrichello   Jordan-Peugeot 196   R
M. Brundle   Jordan-Peugeot 196   6
30 Jun   FRENCH GP, Magny-Cours
R. Barrichello   Jordan-Peugeot 196   9
M. Brundle   Jordan-Peugeot 196   8
14 Jul   BRITISH GP, Silverstone
R. Barrichello   Jordan-Peugeot 196   4
M. Brundle   Jordan-Peugeot 196   6
28 Jul   GERMAN GP, Hockenheim
R. Barrichello   Jordan-Peugeot 196   6
M. Brundle   Jordan-Peugeot 196   10
11 Aug   HUNGARIAN GP, Hungaroring
R. Barrichello   Jordan-Peugeot 196   6
M. Brundle   Jordan-Peugeot 196   R
25 Aug   BELGIAN GP, Spa-Francorchamps
R. Barrichello   Jordan-Peugeot 196   R
M. Brundle   Jordan-Peugeot 196   R
8 Sep   ITALIAN GP, Monza
R. Barrichello   Jordan-Peugeot 196   5
M. Brundle   Jordan-Peugeot 196   4
22 Sep   PORTUGUESE GP, Estoril
R. Barrichello   Jordan-Peugeot 196   R
M. Brundle   Jordan-Peugeot 196   9
13 Oct   JAPANESE GP, Suzuka
R. Barrichello   Jordan-Peugeot 196   9
M. Brundle   Jordan-Peugeot 196   5

1997

9 Mar   AUSTRALIAN GP, Melbourne
R. Schumacher   Jordan-Peugeot 197   R
G. Fisichella   Jordan-Peugeot 197   R

30 Mar   BRAZILIAN GP, Interlagos

R. Schumacher   Jordan-Peugeot 197   R

G. Fisichella   Jordan-Peugeot 197   8

13 Apr   ARGENTINIAN GP, Buenos Aires

R. Schumacher   Jordan-Peugeot 197   3

G. Fisichella   Jordan-Peugeot 197   R

27 Apr   SAN MARINO GP, Imola

R. Schumacher   Jordan-Peugeot 197   R

G. Fisichella   Jordan-Peugeot 197   4

11 May   MONACO GP, Monte Carlo

R. Schumacher   Jordan-Peugeot 197   R

G. Fisichella   Jordan-Peugeot 197   6

25 May   SPANISH GP, Barcelona

R. Schumacher   Jordan-Peugeot 197   R

G. Fisichella   Jordan-Peugeot 197   9/FL

15 Jun   CANADIAN GP, Montreal

R. Schumacher   Jordan-Peugeot 197   R

G. Fisichella   Jordan-Peugeot 197   3

29 Jun   FRENCH GP, Magny-Cours

R. Schumacher   Jordan-Peugeot 197   6

G. Fisichella   Jordan-Peugeot 197   9

13 Jul   BRITISH GP, Silverstone

R. Schumacher   Jordan-Peugeot 197   5

G. Fisichella   Jordan-Peugeot 197   7

27 Jul   GERMAN GP, Hockenheim

R. Schumacher   Jordan-Peugeot 197   5

G. Fisichella   Jordan-Peugeot 197   11

10 Aug   HUNGARIAN GP, Hungaroring

R. Schumacher   Jordan-Peugeot 197   5

G. Fisichella   Jordan-Peugeot 197   R

24 Aug   BELGIAN GP, Spa-Francorchamps

R. Schumacher   Jordan-Peugeot 197   R

G. Fisichella   Jordan-Peugeot 197   2

7 Sep   ITALIAN GP, Monza

R. Schumacher   Jordan-Peugeot 197   R

G. Fisichella   Jordan-Peugeot 197   4

21 Sep   AUSTRIAN GP, Zeltweg

R. Schumacher   Jordan-Peugeot 197   5

G. Fisichella   Jordan-Peugeot 197   4

28 Sep   LUXEMBOURG GP, Nurburgring

R. Schumacher   Jordan-Peugeot 197   R

G. Fisichella   Jordan-Peugeot 197   R

8 Oct   JAPANESE GP, Suzuka

R. Schumacher   Jordan-Peugeot 197   9

G. Fisichella   Jordan-Peugeot 197   7

26 Oct   EUROPEAN GP, Jerez

R. Schumacher   Jordan-Peugeot 197   R

G. Fisichella   Jordan-Peugeot 197   11

Appendix

Jordan – team statistics

BRITISH F3 CHAMPIONSHIP 1981–89 (BEST RESULTS)

1981	–	5	David Leslie
1982	–	5	James Weaver
1983	–	2	Martin Brundle
1984	–	2	Allen Berg
1985	–	9	Harald Huysman
1986	–	2	Maurizio Sandro Sala
1987	–	1	Johnny Herbert
1988	–	8	Paul Warwick
1989	–	4	Rickard Rydell

EUROPEAN F3000 CHAMPIONSHIP 1985–91 (BEST RESULTS)

1988	–	3	Martin Donnelly
1989	–	1	Jean Alesi
1990	–	3	Eddie Irvine
1991	–	7	Damon Hill

GP RECORD TO END OF 1997:

Grands Prix contested:	114
Pole positions:	1
Victories:	0
Second places:	2
Fastest race laps:	2

GP CONSTRUCTORS' CHAMPIONSHIP PLACINGS:

1991	–	5th	13 points
1992	–	11th	1 point
1993	–	9th	3 points
1994	–	5th	28 points
1995	–	6th	21 points
1996	–	5th	22 points
1997	–	5th	33 points

Appendix 3

Jordan –
most successful drivers

RUBENS BARRICHELLO (BR). Born 23.5.72. F1 debut 1993 South Africa (Jordan). Drove for team 1993–96. No victories; one pole position (Spa 1994); one second place (Canada 1995). 46 points for team.

GIANCARLO FISICHELLA (I). Born 14.1.73. F1 debut 1996 Australia (Minardi). Drove for team 1997. No victories; one second place (Spa 1997). 20 points for team.

EDDIE IRVINE (GB). Born 10.11.65. F1 debut 1993 Japan (Jordan). Drove for team 1993–95. No victories; one third place (Canada 1995). 17 points for team.

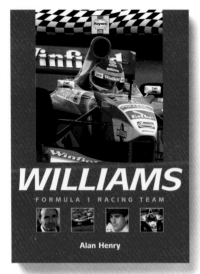

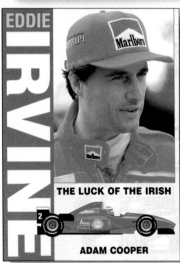

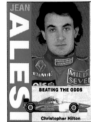
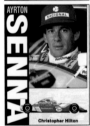